LIVING IN THE HOPE OF *Glory*

Adolphe Monod
(January 21, 1802–April 6, 1856)

LIVING IN
THE HOPE
OF *Glory*

A NEW TRANSLATION
OF A SPIRITUAL CLASSIC

ADOLPHE MONOD

CONSTANCE K. WALKER,
EDITOR AND TRANSLATOR

P&R
PUBLISHING
P.O. BOX 817 • PHILLIPSBURG • NEW JERSEY 08865-0817

Portrait on frontispiece engraved by J. C. Buttre from *Select Discourse* (New York: Sheldon, Blakeman, 1858).

Page design by Lakeside Design Plus
Typesetting by Michelle Feaster

Printed in the United States of America

0-87552-568-7

Contents

CONTENTS

TRANSLATOR'S PREFACE

Many years ago some dear friends gave my husband and me a pamphlet entitled *Looking unto Jesus* by Adolphe Monod.[1] The practical spiritual wisdom of the pamphlet led me to seek out other works by its author, and so I stumbled upon the original 1856 edition of *Les Adieux* (or *Farewells*, here retitled as *Living in the Hope of Glory*).

A Christian classic in France and Switzerland, *Les Adieux* has been blessing its readers for nearly 150 years through numerous French editions and the occasional translation. It comprises a series of short teachings given by Adolphe Monod, a renowned pastor in the Reformed Church of France, during the last six months of his life, as he was suffering from terminal cancer. Yet this is not a book about dying. It is a book about living. It is a book about living wholeheartedly for Christ and living so as to have no regrets at life's end—*Living in the Hope of Glory*.

As I began to read this gem of a book, the riches of practical spiritual wisdom drawn from Monod's life and refined in the "furnace of much affliction" became vibrantly evident, and I longed to share his insights with others. Since no English translation was available, the idea of translating this book myself was born.

---

1 Some sources attribute this work to Théodore Monod.

Though the message of *Les Adieux* is timeless, the passage of one and a half centuries has brought changes to the French and English languages. It has also brought changes in writing styles. Therefore, in this translation, an effort has been made to preserve as much as possible of the general style and phraseology of the original French while still making the message clear and accessible to a modern reader.

The original chronological ordering of the teachings has been modified in order to bring out and build on the structure that Monod introduced in the latter half of *Les Adieux,* where he organized the talks into thematic groups. For those readers wishing to read the talks in their original sequence, there are notes at the end of each chapter pointing to the following week's teaching, as well as a chronological list at the end of this volume.[2] A brief biography of Adolphe Monod has been added, since most modern readers are unacquainted with this extraordinary man. Finally, a few excerpts from the preface to the original 1856 edition explain how the book came into being.

I am deeply grateful for the prayers, encouragement, and helpful suggestions offered to me in this endeavor by friends and family. I especially want to thank

—My husband, Bill, whose quiet patience and expressions of confidence have been a blessing to me throughout

---

2 A sentence that bridged the two series of talks that Monod identified has been omitted because the series no longer follow one another. Also omitted are three cries for help to the Lord that interrupt the flow of the message in a way that seems contrary to Monod's spirit. It is likely that other such cries were uttered but left unrecorded. Finally, there are a few minor differences between the original 1856 edition used for this translation and more recent French editions.

this project, as he shared its ups and downs and provided wise insights along the way;

—Sarah G. Byrd, my special friend and writer of books for young adults, who gave valuable editorial suggestions and feedback, reuniting many a split infinitive;

—David A. Bowen, our friend and trusted pastor, who saw value and new possibilities in *Les Adieux* and started me on the road to finding a publisher;

—Paul E. Engle, friend's friend and publishing world insider, who motivated me to look beyond translation and seek a fresh, more engaging presentation of the content;

—William Edgar, fellow admirer of Adolphe Monod, who graciously offered his linguistic and cultural expertise during the last phases of this project, helping to untie some knotty points of translation; and

—the staff at P&R, teammates in Christ, who embraced this project with enthusiasm and skill while nursing me through a classic case of First Book Syndrome.

Living in the Hope of Glory is not a book to be read in a hurried or hassled state of mind. Rather it is a book to be absorbed and pondered and prayed over so that it may speak to our hearts and our spirits as well as to our minds. It is my prayer that the gracious God who so clearly guided the original teachings may also have guided the translation and that the Holy Spirit will make the pages of this book come alive and bless a new generation of readers.

Constance K. Walker

January 21, 2002

ADOLPHE MONOD: GOD'S ELOQUENT SHEPHERD

"Oh, cross of preaching the cross!" What a strange declaration from the man who was widely regarded as the foremost preacher in nineteenth-century France and Switzerland. Adolphe Monod[1] was a man with a shepherd's heart who longed to be able to spend more time on the pastoral side of his ministry, yet he regarded preaching as a sacred obligation that required his very best effort and preparation. Perhaps this same shepherd's heart—a deep concern for the souls of his hearers—helped make his preaching so effective. It is certainly an important element in *Les Adieux,* which has endured for nearly 150 years as a classic of French evangelical literature.[2]

Adolphe Monod was a man of deep faith and firm doctrine coupled with real warmth and humility of spirit. But as with many of God's most effective servants, he went through intense spiritual struggles early on in his life and ministry. His story can encourage many, even today.

---

1 Pronounced Ah-DOLF Mon-OH.
2 This edition of *Les Adieux* has been retitled *Living in the Hope of Glory* to reflect the book's content rather than the circumstances that led to its existence.

A GODLY HERITAGE

The Monods were an international family. Born in Denmark, brought up in France, and educated in his family's native Switzerland, Adolphe once wrote, "I have three homelands, which is to say I have none." Adolphe's grandfather, Gaspard-Joël Monod, was a pastor in Geneva and Guadeloupe. Adolphe's father, Jean, met his wife, Louise, in Copenhagen and later worked there as a pastor while he began rearing his family. Adolphe-Louis-Frédéric-Théodore Monod, their sixth child, was born on January 21, 1802. After the birth of two more children, the family moved to Paris in 1808 and finally grew to include eight sons and four daughters.

Though large, the Monod family was closely knit. In spite of his many ministry responsibilities, Jean directed the education of his sons, four of whom followed him into the ministry. His own teaching was supplemented by private tutors and by courses at two of the colleges in Paris. For her part, Louise maintained close relationships with each of her children, and in later years her sons corresponded faithfully with her, candidly sharing their struggles and triumphs.

Adolphe, early noted for his intelligence, cheerfulness, and imagination, also showed an unusual aptitude for writing and speaking. Yet he himself was largely unaware of these gifts and remained a genuinely humble person.

THE NEED FOR PERSONAL FAITH

Although Adolphe Monod came from a family of Protestant ministers, his was no easy or automatic ascent to faith. Even after entering the ministry, he struggled long and hard before truly grasping the message and power of the gospel and before fully embracing the evangelical faith that he had long sensed to be true.

Adolphe received his call to the ministry at age fourteen and never doubted its validity, even during his times of spiritual crisis. He and his brothers pursued their theological studies in Geneva, where they were welcomed by family members and friends. The faith of the oldest, Frédéric, came vibrantly alive there as he was swept up in the first Awakening, and he was to remain a strong guiding influence on his brothers. Yet by the time Adolphe and Guillaume (called Billy) arrived in Geneva in 1820, Frédéric had already left, as had Robert Haldane, the Scotsman who had been instrumental in his life. The first great wave of the Awakening had also passed. Thus Adolphe was, for a while, tossed around by various winds of doctrine, wandering through a spiritual wilderness. It was not a question of abandoning Christianity but of finding his place within it and, more importantly, of finding his place in Christ. The journey was to last seven long years.

Always careful, always thorough and striving for excellence, Adolphe was at first happy to take his time in sorting through the issues rather than risk going astray. Then another Scotsman, Thomas Erskine, arrived and was a powerful witness for experiencing the very presence of God. Adolphe's interest was aroused. He could sense the power and truth in the Awakening but was unable to embrace it for himself, and his frustrations mounted.

Aware of his lack and yet certain of his call to the ministry, Adolphe accepted ordination at the end of his studies in 1824. As was common in that era, he did not immediately accept a pastoral position but pursued further studies in

Paris, hoping that this would bring him clarity. He especially wanted to spend time delving into Scripture. Yet, in spite of his efforts and his respect for the Awakening, his spiritual struggle went on.

FROM DARKNESS TO LIGHT

On a trip through Italy in 1826, Adolphe found a group of French-speaking Protestants in Naples who had no church, no pastor, and no means of worship. He gathered them together, agreeing to be their interim pastor, but soon found his spiritual struggle escalating into a crisis. The strain of preaching a gospel that was not real to him—though he fervently desired it to be real—produced inner turmoil, causing him to alternately intensify and abandon his search for clarity. At one point early in 1827, convinced that he had lost his faith, he was ready to leave the ministry, but friends dissuaded him. Recognizing that he could not leave a new congregation without a pastor, he also knew that exposing his doubts to them would only do them harm. Thus he said, "I choose the necessary course, which is still painful to my candor, of preaching what the gospel teaches without considering whether I believe it or not."

Adolphe's family was aware of his inner conflicts, and their concern was both deep and prayerful. His oldest sister, Adèle Babut, living in London, experienced for the third time the death of a dearly loved and only child. In writing to Adolphe, however, her greater concern was for him:

How wrenching is the agony through which I have just passed. . . . I thought of you, dear Adolphe. If my daughter, in her death, could preach to you with

> more eloquence and more conviction than all those who have sought your good, ah, how true it would be to say that the day of her death has greater value than the day of her birth. . . . Adolphe, dear Adolphe, give him your heart. Love him for the good that he has done for me, while waiting for the time when you will love him for the good that he will do for you.

What an amazing family! How could such love and faith and prayer go unanswered for long?

Near the height of this crisis, Thomas Erskine visited Italy and spent many days talking with Adolphe.

> I see in Mr. Erskine and in others a happiness, a peace, an order, a conviction that I totally lack. . . . The creature's perfection can consist only in his relationship with the Creator. Yet—and this is my sin—until this very moment, I have been my own center. I wanted to make my own religion, instead of taking it from God. . . . Only an external influence can save me.

Finally on July 21, 1827, the sun broke through. It is hard to know what, on an earthly plane, finally wrought the dramatic change in Adolphe Monod's life that he had sought for so long, but God's time for him had arrived. Real peace came into his life. "Previously I was without God and burdened with my own well being, while now I have a God who carries the burden for me. That is enough for me." He had been born of the Spirit, and a new inner life began for him— a life that grew over the years and whose maturity can be felt in reading *Living in the Hope of Glory.*

THE TESTING OF HIS FAITH

Shortly after this, at barely twenty-six years of age, he was called to join the pastoral staff of the large Reformed Church of Lyon. As Monod's new faith matured, his preaching took on new clarity and power. He boldly proclaimed the plan of salvation and other biblical truths, which sometimes led him to attack the social injustices of his time. This had the effect of drawing back the evangelicals who had previously left the congregation but also of angering the consistory, the ruling body of the church. First they told him not to preach on salvation by grace. He refused. Then they demanded his resignation. Again he refused. Finally they curtailed his preaching and ministry opportunities, while circulating rumors and petitions to help them in gaining the government's approval to dismiss him.

Then the issue of communion arose. The consistory already knew that Monod was troubled by the lack of adherence in the Lyon church to scriptural and denominational standards on who should eat the Lord's Supper, but the language of his sermon "Who Should Take Communion" was unequivocal and enraging. "I would rather place the body of Christ on a stone and throw the blood of Christ to the winds than deliver them into an unbelieving and profane mouth." They tried to force the issue by requiring Monod to preach and serve communion on Pentecost. In the end, Monod delivered his sermon and left the building prior to the distribution of the elements. The next day, the consistory voted to dismiss him and suspended him from all formal ministry pending the government's decision on his case.

Eventually, in 1832, after three years of unpleasantness, Monod was forced from his position. This was the first time that the government had approved the dismissal of a pastor without specifying a cause—a precedent that disturbed evangelicals all across the country. Through all of this, however, Monod's faith remained solid.

Turning down a teaching position at the new School of Theology in Geneva, he agreed to pastor a group of about seventy people, many of them relatively poor, who had already left the Reformed Church of Lyon. He was encouraged in this by his older brother Frédéric. "The Christians of Lyon must not be abandoned. It is of great importance to show the consistories that if they can remove faithful pastors from the national church, they cannot remove the gospel from those places where it has begun to be preached." Monod was again in the position of establishing a young church, but this time he had the advantage of a strong and tested faith.

YEARS OF FRUITFUL MINISTRY

Adolphe Monod remained at his post for four years as the new congregation grew steadily. Then an offer came that was so manifestly of the Lord that he and his parishioners realized he had to accept it. His call to a professorship at the national church's seminary at Montauban was as unexpected and even improbable as it was unsolicited. Yet Monod was drawn toward teaching and wanted to help return more spiritual life to the Reformed Church of France. As a final confirmation, the Lord provided the right man to take over the shepherding of his flock.

Monod spent over a decade at the Theological Seminary at Montauban, holding professorships first in Gospel Ethics and Sacred Eloquence, and then in Hebrew. Finally, he was appointed to the newly created chair of New Testament Exegesis and Sacred Criticism. These were happy, fruitful years. Freed from the many demands of pastoral ministry, he had more time to spend with his growing family and also a chance to develop his writing skills. Even during this period, however, he regularly found himself occupying the pulpits of local churches and making extended preaching tours during breaks in the academic year. He was becoming something of a voice for French evangelicals. He and his wife also took the unprecedented step of opening their home to the seminary students. This at first led to some consternation and dismay on the part of the students but eventually produced close and helpful relationships.

Adolphe Monod's seminary life was interrupted by another call from God in 1847. The changing climate at Montauban made him sense that his influence there was likely to diminish sharply, and he had begun to think about returning to pastoral ministry. Then, once again through highly improbable and unexpected circumstances, he was offered a position in the Reformed Church of Paris, taking over many of the duties of an aging pastor. There he would join Frédéric on the staff and be close to his mother and other family members. It was something of a homecoming.

But the "cross of preaching the cross" reasserted itself in Monod's life with real vigor. In Paris, the majority of his time was taken up with preparing and delivering sermons. The entire city was organized as one large parish, with tens of thousands of members spread among three houses of worship and served by a team of pastors who shared many of the duties on a rotating basis. Monod's Sunday preaching carried him to far-flung corners of the metropolis. Beginning at 7 a.m., he was called to speak first at a secondary school, then quite often at a prison, and at noon at one of the main churches. In some sense, however, his real parish— the one that gave him the greatest opportunity to guide spiritual lives—was a less formal group started by Frédéric that gathered on Sunday evenings at the Church of the Oratoire.

One year after his arrival in Paris, some of the evangelicals within the denomination withdrew to form the Union of Evangelical Churches. After much earnest prayer, Adolphe remained in the national church to work for change within it, while Frédéric left to become a leader in the new denomination. Still united in their faith, the brothers concluded that the Lord was calling them to do different work, and when the first synod of the new organization was held, Adolphe made a point of inviting all of its members to a gathering in his home. In the end, he was appointed to fill the position in the Reformed Church that Frédéric had just vacated.

Adolphe Monod continued in the pastoral ministry in Paris until his death in 1856.

THE MAN BEHIND THE MESSAGE

In his mature years Adolphe Monod was described by a contemporary as "modest, humble, simple in his appearance and dress." There was a genuineness to his faith and a depth to his love of God that carried through to every part of his life. He was orderly and disciplined, feeling that this would help him be and do his best for his Savior. But above all he was a man of prayer, praying constantly for guidance during sermon preparations and rising early each day to devote himself to meditating on the Word and to prayer.

His personality was reflected in his preaching. He was widely regarded as eloquent, but his was not a flowery rhetoric. It was an eloquence that was designed not to impress but to impart. He expounded the truths of Christianity simply and carefully as they were revealed to him in Scripture. Yet he found ways to do so that made the familiar seem fresh and vivid. He was firm and straightforward but took the time to develop his thoughts with care, always ready to allude to his own need to hear the same truths.

Having grown up in a strong, loving, and Christ-centered home, Adolphe Monod made every effort to pass on those benefits to his children. He married Hannah Honyman while still serving in the Reformed Church at Lyon. Hannah was from a Scottish family residing there, a family to whom Adolphe had ministered. She was well educated, strong in her faith, and simple in her spirit, all of which made her an admirable companion for her husband.

Theirs was a large household. They had three daughters and a son in Lyon and another three daughters (one of whom died at the age of one) during the Montauban years. In addition they looked after a small number of young men entrusted to them for their education. Finally, because of the mild climate of southern France, the Monods invited his sister Adèle Babut and her family to live with them in Montauban as her husband's health was failing. As head of the house, Adolphe took an interest in the welfare of all, including the servants.

Adolphe Monod took parenting seriously. He was strict but fair, never disciplining unjustly or capriciously or in the heat of anger. In addition to concerning himself with the children's general education, he taught them—by precept and example—to value humility, discipline, and hard work, and to heed God's call to holiness and devotion. Though normally somewhat reserved, he knew how to make himself available to his children, taking time each day to join in their games. He was deeply loved and respected, but he was also fun to be with.

Adolphe Monod's public ministry and earthly life were cut off when he was still in his middle fifties. He died from cancer of the liver. Yet the ministry that he had from his sickbed during the last six months of his illness, the ministry of *Les Adieux,* has perhaps had a greater effect on the evangelical church than all of his earlier labors. It was not the ministry he would have chosen, yet because it came to him directly from the hand of God, he accepted it as the more important ministry, which it turned out to be. A week before his death he said, "I have a Savior! He has freely saved me through his shed blood, and I want it to be known that I lean uniquely on that poured-out blood. All my righteous acts, all my works that have been praised, all my preaching that has been appreciated and sought after—all that is in my eyes only filthy rags."[3]

---

3 Much of the information for this brief biography came from *Adolphe Monod, Souvenirs de sa Vie* (Recollections of His Life), published by his family in 1885 and told largely through excerpts from correspondence and diaries. A secondary source is the account of his life by B. Decorvet and E. G. Léonard in the French edition of *Les Adieux* printed in 1978 and published by Editions des Groupes Missionaires (Annemasse, Haut Savoie, France). A biographical note at the beginning of *Select Discourses,* published in 1858 by Sheldon, Blakeman and Co. (New York), and the brief sketch at the beginning of *Looking unto Jesus* were also consulted.

THE STORY OF
LES ADIEUX

Adolphe Monod was taken up from the church on April 6, 1856, after a two-year illness. This was a period marked by suffering that increased continually in intensity and continuity. The talks that will be read here were given in the fall of 1855 and the winter of 1856, from the time he learned that his illness was incurable right up to the day marked by God as the end of his preaching and his suffering.

Mr. Monod and his family learned of the gravity of his illness near the end of September 1855. From that moment on, without ever losing either the hope or the desire of seeing the Lord accomplish in him that for which human art no longer hoped, he peacefully prepared himself to move on, should that be the will of God, and sensed the need to hold himself still closer to his Lord. When a friend and fellow minister spoke to him of communion "as a much neglected and very powerful means of grace" and advised him to partake abundantly, he resolved to take communion each Sunday and to allow those of his friends who expressed the desire to do so to take turns in sharing it.

But he wanted to do even more. Twice within several

days he had been able to give his family a somewhat extended exhortation.[1] Encouraged by this, he thought that the Sunday communion would offer him the occasion each week to exhort a small audience of friends. The first of these Sunday Gatherings took place on October 14, 1855, and they continued without interruption until March 30, 1856.

The wideness of Mr. Monod's spirit made him not only a man of *his* church but also of the whole faithful church. All those who shared his faith, whatever their particular denomination, were brothers to him, and pastors of the Reformed, Lutheran, Independent, and Wesleyan churches took turns presiding at the feast of brotherly love. In this way the sweetness of working for the gospel was augmented by the sweetness of working for "that church of the future which we all anticipate."

The service was celebrated in the patient's bedroom. A table placed near the bed held the bread and the cup. The officiating pastor took his place in front of the table, while Mr. Monod's family with a small number of friends occupied the places around him. An effort was made to vary the group and thus to receive, in turn, all those who had asked to come. An invocation, a song, a prayer, the distribution of the elements—such was the order of service. When the Lord's Supper had been served, Mr. Monod would begin to speak. During the last four gatherings, however, his strength no longer permitted him to have his listeners in his bedroom for a full hour. They had to stand close to his bed in order to hear his exhortation and then move to an adjoining room to

---

1 On learning of the doctor's verdict, Adolphe Monod's eleven siblings gathered in Paris to see him. It was the first time that they had all been together since the marriage of their eldest sister, Adèle Babut, decades earlier.

celebrate communion, with the elements being brought to him by the officiating pastor.

Mr. Monod's voice at this time had a tone of peaceful serenity, of deep Christian love for those whom he exhorted, and often of energy and penetrating eloquence that can be described or felt only by those who were there during his last days.

Since he could not stand the work of a long preparation, he at first contented himself with meditating for a few minutes on the ideas that he planned to develop. Later, seeing that his life was prolonged, he decided to collect the next addresses under a common theme. From this came two series of discourses. In the first, under the title "A Dying Man's Regrets," he gave advice drawn from his experience.[2] In the other, he made known the principal "Results" (or convictions) regarding his faith to which his experience had led him.[3] He began preparing these with greater care, dictating some rather extensive notes, but he soon saw that this method tired him too much in his effort to follow his arguments through to their conclusion. Thus, after the four talks in February he reverted to his previous method.

It is amazing that Mr. Monod was able to stand the fatigue of a one-hour gathering around his bed each Sunday, as well as that of preparing and giving a discourse—even one of only several pages—since he was suffering night and day from pain that was almost always severe and often extreme. But each Sunday, as each day, God gave him the measure of relief or the measure of patience and energy that was required. Even so, the hours following the service were often

2 Now part 5, Avoiding Regrets.
3 Now part 2, My Deepest Convictions.

his most painful ones. He knew it but said, "It is a sacrifice which I willingly offer to God."

On March 2, one month before his death, he prayed, "May God deign to sustain me right to the end and to grant me, if possible (for I am careful to make no demands of him), the grace to cease proclaiming his name only when I cease to live." This request was granted. On March 30, he gathered his small remaining strength to glorify the eternal and infinite love of God and finished his earthly preaching with a prayer of thanksgiving. He died one week later, before the hour for the service had arrived.

From the beginning of the Sunday Gatherings, Mr. Monod's children took on the job of recording his teachings, relying on memory and extensive notes. This work was at first done without Mr. Monod being aware of it. The only one he read over was the twentieth,[4] and though he corrected it with care, he also added that he was astonished to find his words so faithfully reproduced. It is hoped that this volume will serve to the glory of God and the furtherance of his kingdom. May the reader, while preserving the memory of the man to whom we owe this beautiful testimony to the power of faith, look to him from whom proceeds every excellent grace and every perfect gift.

"Let us not forget," said Mr. Monod on Sunday evening, March 2, "to water with our prayers what we have thus planted in the name of the Lord, and let us ask him not to permit a sterile curiosity or even a purely human affection to supplant the pure desire to glorify God, either in him who speaks or him who listens." It is in this spirit that we offer this volume to the people of God. May they, too, greet it in this spirit, with a holy jealousy to ascribe all glory to him who gives every good gift.

4 Now chapter 4 on page 26.

part 1

THE SOURCE OF OUR FAITH

O, the deep, deep love of Jesus—
Vast, unmeasured, boundless, free,
Rolling as a mighty ocean
In its fullness over me.
Underneath me, all around me,
Is the current of God's love,
Leading onward, leading homeward,
To my glorious rest above.
                    Samuel Trevor Francis
                    1834–1925

At a time of great difficulty, Adolphe Monod turned first of all to the source of his faith—an infinite and limitless, loving God whose plans and provision for our salvation are revealed to us in uncompromising terms through his infallible Word.

MEASURELESS WORD, MEASURELESS GOD

(October 14, 1855)

> God made him who had no sin to be sin for us, so that in him we might become the righteousness of God.
>
> 2 Corinthians 5:21

My dear friends, beloved brothers and sisters, I am so happy and grateful to be able to receive with you the body and blood of our Savior—that flesh which is "real food" and that blood which is "real drink" (see John 6:55) for those who receive them in faith by the Holy Spirit.

There is one characteristic of Scripture that would, by itself, be sufficient to identify it as the Word of God: everything in it is ideal. There is nothing in Scripture but the absolute and the perfect. It never dreams of calling us to a certain measure of holiness by a certain measure of faith. All measure is contrary to the instinct of the Bible because it is contrary to God.

The ideal of Scripture is not at all like that of poets, who take the things of this world in order to raise them to the third heaven. Scripture does just the opposite. In it the visible things are only types of the invisible, which alone are real, and it considers all things from God's point of view. This statement struck me this morning as I was reflecting before the Lord on what I could say to you about communion and about the cross of Jesus Christ, in which alone we find remission of sins.

IDEAL SIN

Everywhere Scripture presents us with ideal sin. There is not one of us who has any idea of the horror and crime of sin before God. We have always lived in an atmosphere so saturated with sin, on this earth that drinks iniquity like water and eats it like bread, that we no longer know how to discern the sin that engulfs us from every side.

Here, in a few words, is my experience. We find in the Bible this statement, "At one time we too were foolish, disobedient, deceived and enslaved by all kinds of passions and pleasures. We lived in malice and envy, being hated and hating one another" (Titus 3:3). For a long time it was impossible for me to agree with that statement, which seemed to me to be clearly marked by exaggeration. I confess that even after God, in his grace, had turned my heart to him on the day that he had set from time eternal, I was for a long while still unable to accept it completely. What is more, I confess that ever since, and even today, I cannot comprehend it in its fullness. Yet I am convinced that it is perfectly true and that if I have not really grasped it in my experience, the fault is entirely mine.

It is just here that I have understood the necessity of a witness existing before, outside of, and above us. I accept that statement from Titus 3:3 as coming from God because I find it in his Word, and I beseech him to finish revealing its meaning to me by his Spirit. By God's grace I have come—not year by year, things don't go that fast, but from one interval of several years to another—to see this doctrine more clearly and to sense its truth more forcefully in my heart. I am convinced that when the veil of this flesh has fallen, I will recognize that this is the most faithful painting and the portrait with the greatest likeness that was ever drawn of my heart—and by this I mean my natural heart.

Let us ask God to reveal to us our sinful state, yet without pressing him too hard, because he knows full well that if he made us grow in that knowledge faster than in the knowledge of his mercy we would fall into despair.

IDEAL PARDON

But pardon is also depicted to us everywhere in Scripture as ideal. If only part of our sins were pardoned; if out of a thousand sins or a million sins (if our sins could be counted) only one were left that was not dealt with, then that pardon would be useless to us. But our pardon is complete.

The passage that was cited a moment ago (2 Cor. 5:21) is one of my favorites. Jesus Christ did not simply make atonement for some sins, he made atonement for sin itself. He was not considered to be a sinner, he was made to be sin; and, mystery of mysteries, the full curse of God was gathered together on that innocent, holy head. Likewise, we are not simply made righteous in him, we are made to be righteousness itself, in such a way that when God looks at us in Jesus Christ he sees us as his own beloved Son and finds in us everything that could attract his gaze and his kindness.

We who believe have been given by God to Jesus Christ as the recompense for his sacrifice. He can no more break his word to us than to Jesus Christ, and all of his perfection is so thoroughly committed in this relationship that this gift of his infinite mercy becomes like a right due to us by virtue of our perfect righteousness in Jesus Christ.

Even the terms used in Scripture to show us the nature of sin before God also show us how he has blotted out our sins. He has "put all my sins behind [his] back" (Isa. 38:17) as if he were afraid of seeing them again; he "will hurl all our iniquities into the depths of the sea" (Micah 7:19); he has "swept away [our] offenses like a cloud, [our] sins like the morning mist" (Isa. 44:22). Here we see what it is for God to forget sin. The Lord is shown to us as making an effort to forget, or rather not to forget but to eradicate.

IDEAL SANCTIFICATION

Finally, Scripture is ideal in what it says to us about sanctification. We have no idea what Scripture demands of us and the degree of holiness to which we can and must attain. What fullness there is in this verse: "May God himself, the God of peace, sanctify you through and through. May your whole spirit, soul and body be kept blameless at the coming of our Lord Jesus Christ" (1 Thess. 5:23). And in order to prove to us that this is not simply a wish, the apostle immediately adds, "The one who calls you is faithful and he will do it" (1 Thess. 5:24). It is no more possible for him to refuse us this grace than it is for us to conceive of him breaking his word.

And how can we arrive at this holiness? Consider the holy men the Bible gives us as examples. How were they great? It was not by their enlightenment or by their natural gifts but by their faith. Look at Saint James (James 5:16). In order to show us the power of faith and of prayer, he takes perhaps the most miraculous man in the Bible in the most miraculous of his miracles. He gives us the boldness of that prayer by Elijah as something completely natural and offers him as an example to the smallest, to the most humble, in order to show us what the fervent prayer (literally, the "energetic" prayer) of a righteous man can do.

A NEEDED PERSPECTIVE

If we were able, each one of us, beginning today, to sense in our heart the enormity of our sin, the fullness of our pardon, and the power of the holiness to which we must attain, what a change in our life, what a healthy influence for the church itself!

PRAYER

Oh, God! You who know all of the evil and suffering that sin has brought on our poor earth and on this poor humanity, you who see all that is being suffered at this very moment and that we could not stand to look at, we lift up to you all those who are afflicted so that you might pour out on them the treasures of your grace and consolation. We cannot name them all to you, but you yourself know their names.

We lift up to you the victims of war—so many families

7

deep in mourning and so many others who live in continual anxiety. We lift up to you those who are oppressed and persecuted for righteousness' sake. We lift up to you the slaves; think of these thousands, these millions of slaves oppressed by men who profess your name, by servants of Christ who are not servants. We lift up to you the poor—ah, the poor!—the sick, the sick who are poor.

We lift up to you all those who know you, that you would sustain them and pour out on them your peace and your comfort. And as for those who don't know you, we commend them to your grace so that you might reveal yourself to them, because if they do not possess you, their only other alternative is despair.

As for me who suffers a little, I confess Christ and his peace. I thank you for the joy that you have poured into my soul. You will call us, perhaps, to be separated for a little while, but what is that? We know that by your grace we will all one day be reunited close to you.

To read the talks in original
chronological order, go to
chapt. 8 on p. 59.

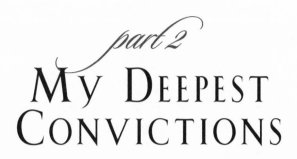

MY DEEPEST CONVICTIONS

*My hope is built on nothing less
Than Jesus' blood and righteousness;
I dare not trust the sweetest frame,
But wholly lean on Jesus' name.*

*On Christ the solid rock I stand—
All other ground is sinking sand,
All other ground is sinking sand.*

Edward Mote
1797–1874

his series of talks deals with the substance of Adolphe Monod's faith. He wanted his friends and family to be certain about the convictions that had guided him through life and that sustained him in death—convictions that only grew stronger through his years of ministry. But these are not dry doctrinal statements. They are warmly personal and decidedly practical.

These talks were originally given much later in *Les Adieux* but have been moved forward in the present edition in order to establish the nature of Monod's faith before considering his words on living out that faith. If you find parts of the first teaching in the group to be a bit heavy, press on! It only enhances the sweetness of what follows.

Rescue from the Depths of Sin

(December 16, 1855)

"There is no one righteous, not even one;
    there is no one who understands,
    no one who seeks God.
All have turned away,
    they have together become worthless;
there is no one who does good, not even one."

But now a righteousness from God, apart from the law, has been made known, to which the Law and the Prophets testify. This righteousness from God comes through faith in Jesus Christ to all who believe. There is no difference, for all have sinned and fall short of the glory of God, and are justified freely by his grace through the redemption that came by Christ Jesus.

Romans 3:10–12, 21–24

My dear friends, this communion places before our eyes a remembrance of the deepest joy that ever was. But let us not forget that just as Jesus Christ walked toward glory and toward the resurrection by the cross, so this joy can be felt only by those who have first sensed the bitterness of sin. Indeed, our joy is in proportion to the acuteness with which we have sensed that bitterness.

Oh, my friends, what is sin? Who is there among us who understands what he has of the criminal, what he has of the bitter within him? Who among us understands the awful judgment that he naturally draws upon himself? Who among us understands the absolute necessity of being completely washed and set free in order to taste even a moment of rest? It seems to me that meditating in a special way on the depths of sin belongs to those who live particularly immersed in suffering and who are called to ponder constantly this mystery of a God full of love who sends suffering upon suffering to his children.

Sin in the Life of a Mature Christian

Take a man like François Gonthier of Nyon. As for me, I have never known a man who, as far as one can tell, had progressed further in true, solid Christian piety of the sort that unites purity of faith with a spirit of humility and love. And yet, this man, who seemed as if he ought to be filled with all of the consolations of God, was filled with all his bitterest provisions. He lost, in succession, an only son, a tenderly beloved wife, and a twelve-year-old daughter who alone recalled his lost treasures to him. Left alone, it was needful that the hand of God make that solitude even deeper by lifting from him first a well-loved sister and then a young niece of twenty years upon whom all of his affections had been concentrated. And I have not mentioned all that he lost. Add to that a health so profoundly altered that he said to me one day, "Do you know how I write my books? In the way one gets the essence from an orange rind, by squeezing on it so that after a while the essence comes out drop by drop." He had been given over to excessive weakness and to almost continual pain. This pain kept increasing along with the weakness, and all these troubles grew ever greater until the end of his life. When I think of an existence like that, I say to myself, "What is sin?"

I know very well that someone could say to me that a man like Gonthier is smitten so that his afflictions might instruct the church through the patience and meekness with which he bears them, and that is certainly his greatest consolation, because that is his greatest resemblance to Jesus Christ. Nevertheless, God would not have sent all those sufferings to Gonthier solely in the interest of others. We must not confuse the creature with the Creator, for God would thus be making the man into a savior. When it comes to Jesus Christ, God smites him for the sins of man, but when it comes to one of us, God never smites him with a measure of suffering that his personal sins have not merited.

The point is that sin merits a great deal more than what we suffer or even than what we can imagine suffering. That is what we learn from Scripture and in particular from every page of the psalms. David cannot deal with the subject of his suffering without sliding, as if without noticing it, into the subject of his sins. You can see this particularly in rereading Psalm 38, where he repeatedly mixes his suffering with his sins to such an extent that one scarcely knows how to distinguish them. What then is sin? What horror does it offer to

13

God's eyes? What is the agony it necessitates? What is the ransom that can atone for it?

SIN IN THE LIFE OF AN ORDINARY CHRISTIAN

Next consider sin in the life of an ordinary Christian who has never elevated himself to as strong and effective a Christian life as that of Gonthier; who goes through life somehow or other without dishonoring his calling but who hasn't sensed the bitterness of sin. He has his afflictions because one always has them, but he hasn't known how to turn his afflictions into a cross and unite his sufferings with those of his Savior.

Look into the heart of such a Christian (who may still be a sincere man) and see all that is there of latent sin, hidden decay, and secret infection. If this heart came to be suddenly laid open before us, it would cause in us a fearful horror, provided that we possessed the ability to sense the horror of sin, which is to say the ability to understand all the holiness of the law of God and all that the holiness of this formidable law requires.

SIN IN THE LIFE OF A NONBELIEVER

Then consider sin in the people of the world who are immersed in it. They have done nothing since coming into the world but drink sin as water and breathe it as air. On the inside they are entirely made up of sin, while spiritually they are surrounded by a crust of sin that no ray of life-giving, healthy, sanctifying light has ever penetrated! What an abyss, what a tomb, what a sight before the eyes of God. Men, thousands and millions of men spread out over the face of the earth in whom is found nothing but this frightful sin. They have at most a vague awareness of it that comes from time to time from God to beg them to be converted, but they remain plunged in that state that is so dreadful and abominable before God.

Sin in the best Christians, sin in ordinary Christians, sin in the church, and sin in the world. Oh, my friends, what misery! What is sin!

GOD'S VIEW OF SIN

Sin is what Jesus Christ saw when he descended from heaven to save us. We didn't know it, but he knew it. We didn't sense it, but he sensed it for us. This is what gave him the strength to bear the agony of the cross along with the pains of Gethsemane, the battles in the wilderness, and all the humiliations that preceded it and of which his entire life seems to be formed. And now the sufferings that he endured for us must become for us the measure of what it is for him to look on sin and of the depth of the abyss from which he has drawn us.

None of us has any idea; no, my friends, none of us has any idea of what sin is! Not one of us understands sin because not one of us fully knows the Savior—neither his sufferings nor his love. Oh, my friends, in the presence of this shed blood and this broken flesh, let us learn what sin is and what the peril to our souls is in order that we might take refuge close to Jesus and seek in him alone that which he alone can give us.

Let us settle it in our hearts that we will never learn the nature of sin except from Holy Scripture. Never will our personal meditations reveal it to us. This is a point on which I especially sense the need for and the reality of the inspiration and divine authority of Scripture, because we would never have learned to know sin except through obedience. We would never have learned without an authority outside of and superior to ourselves, independent of our inner feelings. We must, without doubt, work on it through study, meditation, and fervent prayer, but the luminous truth comes from on high, given most especially by the Spirit of God speaking with the authority of God. For we must begin by receiving the horror of sin at a time when we are still incapable of feeling it for ourselves.

THE RESCUE FROM SIN

Very well then, my friends, let us throw ourselves into the arms of the Savior. Shall the sufferings and pains of this earth hold us back? Do we really have the time to busy ourselves with them when it is a matter of saving our souls! Let us go to Jesus with a sense of deep humiliation but also with an unreserved confidence in the One who has accomplished all and suffered all for us.

Oh, the infinite sweetness of resting ourselves fully at the foot of his cross! I begin to understand the extent of my misery, but I embrace the cross of my Savior. I desire only it and its unique grace and righteousness with no mixture of my works. My works! They could do nothing but condemn me. But redeemed by him, washed in his blood, which made atonement for my sins, I take hold of his cross, and I lean solely on the sacrifice of my Savior.

And then let us speak of the Savior to those who do not know him. Given such an evil that, unlike all the evils of earth, is the only true evil and the principle behind all of the others; and given such a remedy in our hands that, unlike all the remedies of earth, is the only sure and infallible one, can we really go through life, society, our families, our neighbors, our friends without speaking to them of sin and of Jesus Christ, who is their Savior and ours?

Let us take hold of the cross, proclaim the cross. Let us die while embracing it, die while proclaiming it, and our death will be the beginning of life. God will be glorified in our bodies whether by life or by death, and above all by the blood and the redemption of the Lamb of God. That is what I ask of God for each of you as I do for myself, in the love of Christ that I beg him to increase toward us. Amen.

To read the talks in original
chronological order, go to
chapt. 17 on p. 110.

THE TWO NATURES
OF CHRIST

(February 17, 1856)

Philip said, "Lord, show us the Father and that will be enough for us."

Jesus answered: "Don't you know me, Philip, even after I have been among you such a long time? Anyone who has seen me has seen the Father. How can you say, 'Show us the Father'? Don't you believe that I am in the Father, and that the Father is in me? The words I say to you are not just my own. Rather, it is the Father, living in me, who is doing his work. Believe me when I say that I am in the Father and the Father is in me."

John 14:8–11a

Considering what we have just done in recalling all that God has given us in his beloved Son, one would like to remain silent or to add only words of worship and thanksgiving to this solemn service. But, since the Lord has called us also to glorify his Word and to give testimony to its truth, and since in certain situations the opportunities to do so are quite rare, I will continue to open to you the truth such as it is in my heart. I do so, relying on God's help, while waiting for the day when the Lord will shut my mouth and say to me, "That is enough. You have spoken enough. Go now, and rest from your works in the bosom of your Savior."

I feel called, in this particular situation and, above all, in these dark and troubled days in which we live, to give testimony of the convictions to which the Christian life and the experience of pastoral ministry have led me in my infirmity, so that the sentiments with which I will enter my rest and go to sleep when God calls me may be well known. I want there to be no shadow of doubt in the hearts of my friends, my brothers, or the church about what now causes and will (I hope, through the goodness of God) increasingly cause the assurance of my soul.

There is one first essential thing on which I will not dwell now because we discussed it at some length just recently. I know that my small audience changes, but I can only follow a certain order in the thoughts that I communicate to you. That first item is sin.[1] The main point is to have a clear, deep sense of our state of sinfulness before God, not only through our present conviction that we have sinned against his holy law, but because we have begun to measure

1 The message recorded in the previous chapter, "Rescue from the Depths of Sin," was recognized by Adolphe Monod to have been part of this series on his convictions but was originally given before he began to organize his addresses by theme. In the present edition, all the parts of the series are gathered together.

the enormity of sin, the terror of God's judgments, and the depth of the abyss from which we had to be drawn.

Once we have been pierced by that bitterness of sin that is without decrease, without excuse, and without any explanation, and once we content ourselves with saying, "Against you, you only, have I sinned" (Ps. 51:4), then the entire gospel is summed up for us in a single word, or rather in a single name: Jesus Christ. In particular, that is how it is summed up right now for me. Likewise, Saint Paul says to us, "For I resolved to know nothing while I was with you except Jesus Christ and him crucified" (1 Cor. 2:2).

WHO IS THIS JESUS CHRIST?

Who *is* Jesus Christ? What is he? What impression do you have of him? How would you reply to his question "Who do people say I am?" (Mark 8:27). That point is the foundation and the starting point of our faith. . . .

When we consider Jesus Christ, we look at him first of all as a man, but we soon notice that this is no ordinary man. We find here an infinite charity, a goodness always ready to come to our aid, and a power always able to deliver us. We find a master and a liberator who heals the sicknesses of the body in order to demonstrate that he can heal those of the soul—even the deepest, most invisible miseries. We find a holiness without spot, a holiness which is that of God himself transported to earth. In a word, what we find in a man's body and a man's spirit is a godlike virtue of truth, strength, goodness, and deliverance that no man has ever possessed or even suspected. We find a virtue that draws us to him as to the one whom we instinctively sense can alone bring us all the deliverance we need.

Very soon, though, as we listen to Scripture and listen to
Jesus himself, this mystery begins to grow clearer. Yet it does
so through an even deeper mystery. We learn that our Lord
Jesus Christ—for such is the man we have just been considering—born in a supernatural birth, is not only Son of man
but at the same time also Son of God: Son of man, which is
to say man; Son of God, which is to say God. If he has a
virtue, a power, a holiness, and a goodness that are divine, it
is because he is God. He is the image of God's person and
the splendor of his majesty, "for in Christ all the fullness of
the Deity lives in bodily form" (Col. 2:9). This is the mystery of piety: God manifested in the flesh, God being able to
say to his disciples (as we heard it read earlier), "Anyone
who has seen me has seen the Father" (John 14:9).

I have a deep and growing conviction about this, my
dear friends, that is shared by all faithful people from earli-
est times right up to the end. It is shared by the prophets to
the extent that it was given them to catch a glimpse of it; by
patriarchs, apostles, witnesses, and martyrs; by faithful
church fathers, reformers, and servants of the Lord of all
ages. This is quite simply the key to the evangelical building
and the foundation of the whole gospel. It is from this starting point that all the infinite paths diverge toward all the acts
of faith and obedience to which we may be called.

The entire Christian life rests so completely on this
foundation of Jesus Christ, God made manifest in the flesh,
that apart from it not only is Jesus Christ dethroned, but
God himself is also. The living God lives no more. Instead
we are given a god of the deists, a god of the pantheists, a
god of the rationalists, and of all the other kinds of -ists that
have ever existed in this world. We are given a god who is
only a dead god, one who has never saved or sanctified or

21

consoled a single person. For the true God is the one who reveals himself to us and, more than that, who gives himself to us in Jesus Christ. Someone has said and said so well, "In creation God shows us his hand, but in redemption he gives us his heart."

Jesus Christ is God, and yet Jesus Christ is man, really and truly man, truly and fully God. To many this doctrine seems more speculative than practical, . . . but that is not at all the case. Far from being a speculative doctrine, it is the very basis of Christian life and practice. Likewise Saint Paul, while calling it a mystery, calls it the mystery of godliness: "the mystery of godliness is great" (1 Tim. 3:16). Apart from this doctrine, there is no Christian life, no Christian holiness, no Christian consolation, no Christian strength, no Christian death. It is the foundation of everything else, and the grace of the Lord Jesus poured out in our hearts is our only strength as it is our only hope.

Jesus, My God

That is why I want it to be known and why I confess that in Jesus Christ I behold my God. I bow before him with Thomas, saying, "My Lord and my God!" (John 20:28). With Saint John I give this testimony of him: "He is the true God and eternal life" (1 John 5:20). With Saint Paul I say, "Christ who is God over all, forever praised!" (Rom. 9:5). I honor him as I honor the Father, and I know that the Father, who is so jealous of his own glory, is far from jealous of the glory I give to Jesus Christ. Rather, he approves it as glory given to himself, because he desires "that all may honor the Son just as they honor the Father" (John 5:23).

I strive to live in communion with Jesus Christ and in the

peace of Jesus Christ, praying to him, waiting upon him, speaking to him, listening to him. In short, I bear constant witness to him day and night in a way that would be idolatry if he were not God, and God in the highest and most unique meaning that the human spirit is able to give to that lofty name. Jesus Christ is the one who is: "I am," "I am the way the truth and the life," "I am that I am," "Jehovah," "the Lord God almighty." That is what Jesus Christ is and what he is for me.

If, in the last moments of my life, my illness should keep me from bearing him this witness, I want it to be known that I bear it to him here, and that in giving it to him I have no thought of ever drawing it back from him! I have only known that small amount of faith, of consolation, of holiness, of charity that I possess (and that I ask God to increase) since, in changing my initial impressions, I have learned to worship Jesus Christ as my Savior and my God.

JESUS, MY BROTHER

Having established that, let me say that, at the same time, I find in Jesus Christ my brother, my fellow man, my friend; the one who is with me and near me; the one who, according to that lovely phrase in Psalm 84, is "my sun and shield." My sun is my distant protection, while my shield is my nearby protection. Between this divine Sun and me there are so many things and such an enormous distance (I leave it to others to calculate its physical length, though no one could ever calculate its spiritual length) that I have need of the Lord close at hand, like a shield that covers me on all sides. His heart presses against my heart, and his arms continually surround me, so that I can say to him (and even whisper in his ear, if I so desire, so that no one in the whole world can hear it), "I am yours, and you are mine. I know you are my God and my brother, and you know that I am your child and your servant who, in spite of all his infirmities, believes in you, who never trembles except for believing so little, and who aspires to believe in such a way as to glorify you in his bitterest trials."

Thus Jesus Christ is my brother. What a marvelous blessing to have God for a brother and to have a brother for God! I could never even try to speak of what a deep, tender, and mysterious combination there is in this union of God and man. That is what Jesus Christ is to me.

I cannot say any more at this point, but you see what my thoughts are with reference to the Lord. I would be ready to confess them before his tribunal, if he called me to appear there, knowing that he would not refute me and that the only thing lacking in these feelings is what is lacking in my worship and my gratitude. I am infinitely behind in the feelings of love and adoration that I owe him.

Jesus, My Strength

My friends, that is what Jesus Christ has become for me. That is what God, in his grace, has made him for me. He did so by using, in turn, the diverse means of education, example, action, books, and preaching. He used these various instruments in different ways to bring varying degrees of light, thus establishing me in his grace for all eternity. I know that he prepared me in this way and that he wanted to give me the power to resist what he is sending me today. And what he is sending me today will be the crowning touch of all his dispensations to me, though we cannot really affirm yet that nothing will surpass it.

I urge you to ask yourselves and see if Jesus Christ is for you what he is for the universal faithful church; what he is, I repeat, for the patriarchs, the prophets, the apostles, the martyrs, the church fathers, the reformers, and for all the saints of all ages. See if he is for you what he is according to his Word, according to his own declarations, and according to the witness of the Father. Rest when he is, and never rest until then, for no one should rest until he has learned to rest at the foot of the cross of his Savior God, even if he has to be pushed there by storms and winds and to fall from exhaustion into that place which he would never again desire to leave!

To read the talks in original
chronological order, go to
the next chapter.

THE TWO VOICES OF SCRIPTURE

(February 24, 1856)

Bear in mind that our Lord's patience means salvation, just as our dear brother Paul also wrote you with the wisdom that God gave him. He writes the same way in all his letters, speaking in them of these matters. His letters contain some things that are hard to understand, which ignorant and unstable people distort, as they do the other Scriptures, to their own destruction.

2 Peter 3:15–16

My dear friends in Christ who give me such a great token of your love, those of you who have been present at several of these gatherings know that the thing that I enjoy most when I address these few words to you is to recount the memories of a Christian who believes himself ready to appear before God. I then like to sum up in God's presence and communicate to you the main results of this man's studies of the Word of God and also the convictions in which he desires to finish living and dying. Having in this way shown the results at which I have arrived concerning sin and the person of the Lord Jesus Christ, I come today to speak for a few moments about his Word.

THE VOICE OF THE LORD

I declare, as though before the judgment seat of Jesus Christ, where I expect soon to appear, my unshakable conviction that when Scripture speaks, it is God who speaks. All of my research and my studies, whether of Scripture or church history or my own heart, and all of the discussions that have been raised in these last years on the inspiration and divine authority of God's Word have only strengthened me in this conviction. Throughout my three-phase ministry (three periods of about ten years each, at Lyon, Montauban, and Paris), by pathways that God's wisdom has made somewhat diverse, I have become increasingly convinced that when Scripture speaks, God speaks. When Scripture proclaims God's will or the way of salvation or the great doctrines of sin and grace, and of the Father, Son, and Holy Spirit, what it tells us is no less true and no less certain than if heaven were opened above us at this very moment and the voice of God resounded, as it once did at Sinai, saying these same things to us.

There are no bounds to the trust and submission that we owe the Scriptures, any more than there are limits to the truth and the faithfulness of God. Thus, when the day arrives that I enter into the invisible world (a day of which only

God knows the number and that I long for as for a deliverance without ever daring to hasten it), I do not expect to find things any different from the way in which the Word of God has represented them to me here. Of course there will be the enormous difference in the condition and state of the soul before and after death, in time and in eternity, but, fundamentally, the voice that I will hear then, that will be clothed with full power to judge, that will rule over all creatures—that voice will be the same one that I listen to today on earth. Thus I will say, "That is just what God was saying to me, and how I thank him today that I did not wait until I had seen before believing!"

I have this confidence because Scripture is the divine expression of the truths and maxims that form the very foundation of the invisible and eternal realm. It is like a letter that God has written from the invisible world to his children detained in the visible one, so that henceforth through faith in God they might learn the true nature of things and that, as a result, they might act to bring about the salvation of their souls. Those who believe God will save their souls, but how could those who don't believe God ever save them?

Scripture is thus the Word of God in the highest sense of that expression, but also in the simplest and most familiar sense. It is the only sure rule of faith and life, a rule to which all others must be submitted. All the meetings in the world, all the committees, conferences, prayers, and common quests[1] have no value at all unless each is submitted and subordinated to the sovereign, infallible, unchangeable authority of God's Word.

---

1 The meaning of this phrase is unclear. Perhaps it refers to times when believers gather together to seek God's will through prayer.

The testimony that I bear to Scripture is not just the testimony that is given to it by Moses or David or Saint Paul or Saint John or Augustine or Chrysostom. It is not just the testimony of all the saints of all ages. It is the testimony that is given to it by God himself and by Jesus Christ, who gives to the Word of God the same glory that he receives from it.

Experience and observation, which we are permitted to invoke provided that we do so with humble diffidence, come mercifully to confirm all these testimonies. For never has it been granted to any man or to any group of men to compose a book, even a very short book, that equals Holy Scripture and that could produce the same effects of comfort, sanctification, and conversion. Never *will* it be granted to any man or group of men unless the Holy Spirit guides them in the same special way that he guided the apostles and prophets.

It is not a question of personal holiness, for the holiness we have just recognized in Scripture is no less present in the words of Saint Paul than in the words of Jesus Christ. Rather it is a question of divine direction. That direction is even more apparent when one considers that this book was written in a completely historical order and that, in spite of being spread out over nearly two thousand years, it still has a coherent and consistent doctrine on each point.

The Bible is a book apart, which no other ever has or ever could equal. It reigns alone over all the systems, all the uncertainties, and all the questions that concern or upset mankind.

THE VOICE OF HIS SERVANTS

But (and here I enter into a new train of thought), no sooner have I, for my part, sanctioned the name Word of God, which the Bible has received from God himself and from Jesus Christ, than in looking closely at this book I find it to be full of man. It contains so many marks of humanity. At first I might even feel a certain fear, as if I had gone too far before in the testimony that I gave it. In effect, I recognize in the writers of this book a marked individuality of style and character. If, by some impossibility, some lost book were to be discovered today that, through some error, had not previously been included in canon, there is no one who is at all versed in the Holy Scriptures who would not be able to say instantly whether it was by Jeremiah or Isaiah; whether it was by Peter, John, or Paul. That is how different these writers were and how clearly each one left the mark of his individual character on all that he wrote.

I also find many things in this book that its writers could have said without the special help of the Spirit of God (for example, 2 Tim. 4:13), and since God does not perform any useless miracles, we see there the spirit of the man, which has its own part in the composition of the Word of God.

There is more. I find touches in Scripture that remind us of human infirmity, as when Paul tries to recollect, without daring to trust his memory, how many people he baptized at Corinth. But he doesn't become preoccupied with the question, "for Christ did not send me to baptize, but to preach the gospel" (1 Cor. 1:17). It was clearly part of God's plan that on each page of this book that we call the Word of God we should also recognize a word of man.

RELATING THE TWO

But if someone who has not reflected on this question can experience a kind of fear, he will not be long in reassuring himself and in seeing, on the contrary, a measure of blessing, light, and spirituality in the human side of the composition of Scripture. In the last analysis, how could it have been avoided? It could have been avoided only if Scripture had been dictated word for word, without any influence from personal character or historical events.

Let us take an extreme example, which I cite with the deepest respect. When God places words of reproof against an unfaithful prophet in the mouth of a dumb animal, it is very clear that his word acts without an intermediary endowed with a will of its own.[2] The "inspiration" (for it surely is one) is that much more visible in this case when the instrument is completely passive. But what in this inspiration of a being deprived of reason can compare with the inspiration of an apostle, infused as it is with his experience and personal feelings? A similar consideration of all the intermediate levels of the activity or passivity of the instrument would reveal that, to the extent that the inspiration becomes more personal, it gains interest without losing any of its authority.

Also, how much more beautiful, how much more touching Scripture is in the way it was given! It was given by God in the course of history through men whose spirits were led by the Spirit of God; men like us who were able to say, "I believed, therefore I spoke" (Ps. 116:10 NKJV). It was given through men of whom it can be said, for example, "Elijah was a man just like us. He prayed earnestly that it would not rain, and it did not rain on the land for three and a half years" (James 5:17).

The Word of God was given in history to men like us. It was not brought by superior, invisible beings but by men weak

2 See the story of Balaam in Numbers 22–24, especially Numbers 22:15–35.

like ourselves and saved like ourselves; by men who were the first to believe and who could say, "I have believed what I exhort you to believe." Because of this, it has a life, a freshness, a power that can touch our hearts all the more deeply. A familiarity and something like a secret friendship forms between those hearts and that Word, so that the most solemn of books is, at the same time, the dearest and most tender. In all this, there is a deep understanding of the human heart and one of the most intimate beauties of the Word of God.

Though it was composed by simple men who did not cease, in writing it, to fight against sin and to depend personally on the faith that they announced, the Bible is no less the Word of God. Rather it is all the more divine for being more human. That is to say that one is more aware of the power and the presence of God's Spirit and of his influence on our souls when, in writing the Bible, God uses those instruments in whom only his Spirit could cause such supernatural light and power to operate, turning them into vessels destined to carry the truth to the very ends of the earth. That is how Holy Scripture gains access to the deepest recesses of our hearts. That is how it teaches us on God's part while, at the same time, it teaches us through men. It joins together simultaneously all the elements capable of touching, of enlightening, of converting to God, of sustaining in the shadows of this age, and of accomplishing all in all.

LIVING WORD AND WRITTEN WORD

There is, my friends (and this is my last thought), a contrast, or rather a comparison that, for the Christian, can clarify everything and confirm what I have just said. It is the view that we had last Sunday and that is given to us throughout Scripture of Jesus Christ uniting in himself the divine nature and human nature in such a marvelous way that we cannot give an account of it, and yet it is the very foundation and the comfort of our faith.

Last Sunday we began by considering Jesus Christ in his human perfection, after which we contemplated him in his divinity. Suppose that we had reversed that order. Suppose that we had spoken first of the divine nature of Jesus Christ and of our obligation to worship him as God, and that we had then gone on to make for the first time the observation that Jesus Christ is a man, able to suffer and die. I do not know what other fear could have slipped itself into our soul as easily as the fear that we had attributed too much divinity to him.

But, as we saw in that same Sunday teaching, Scripture shows us everywhere that perfect divinity is united in him with perfect humanity and that each increases the value of the other without in any way compromising its reality. It even reveals that Jesus is all the more man for being more God and that he is all the more God for being more man. In which moments is Jesus Christ most human? Is it not in the temptation in the desert, in the anguish of Gethsemane, and in the fearful agony of the cross? And are these not also the moments when he is most God? He gains victory over the tempter, overcomes pain, and triumphs over the cross by the power of the Spirit of God that dwells in him, for the Spirit does not dwell in him with measure as he does in us, but without measure, as in the only Son of the Father.

It is the same with the Word of God. It is God's Word, true and eternal, and, at the same time, it is man's word where one senses the gleam of the human spirit and the beat of the human heart. It is precisely in the moments where one best senses (in a Saint Paul or a Saint John, for example) the fight of faith and the persevering struggle against sin that one also senses best how divine is the light diffused into their souls. This light was given first of all that they might battle on their own behalf and then that they might, with divine virtue, diffuse it out into the whole world. That is why we can say that the Word is all the more divine for being more human.

How wonderful this comparison between Jesus Christ and Holy Scripture appears to me! Moreover, you may be sure that it is not a comparison that I dreamed up in my head but one that is furnished to me by God's Word. For someone who knows that it "cannot be broken" (John 10:35), it is enough to recall a most astonishing thing: Scripture sometimes gives the same name to Jesus Christ and to Holy Scripture. It calls them both "Word of God." One of these words, Jesus Christ, is the living Word of God, the personal manifestation of his invisible perfections in the bosom of humanity. The other, Scripture, is the written Word of God, the verbal manifestation, given through language, of these same invisible perfections.

These two are inseparable for us. Jesus Christ is revealed to us only through Scripture, and Scripture is given to us only in order to reveal Jesus Christ. Thus Scripture is the written Word of God just as Jesus Christ is the living Word of God. Those who rely on the human characteristics of Scripture to belittle its divinity use the same sort of reasoning as those who rely on the human personality of Jesus Christ in order to deny him the title of God. They fail to understand that human nature and divine nature are united in the person of Jesus Christ just as the human word and the divine word are united in the Scriptures. It is no more astonishing that Scripture, though the Word of God, should at the same time bear so many marks of humanity than that Jesus Christ, though God, should be man.

As to the way that the two natures fuse together in the one case and the two voices in the other, it is the very essence of faith's object on this point. It is a deep mystery, but, as Saint Paul tells us, "the mystery of godliness" (1 Tim. 3:16). It is a mystery that fills our souls with joy and hope.

OUR RESPONSE TO SCRIPTURE

Yes, Scripture is the unique path by which we can arrive at knowing Jesus Christ without risk of error, just as Jesus Christ is the unique path by which we can arrive at the Father. Yes, if you want to save your souls, you must believe in the Word of God; you must submit to the Word of God. You must not search inside yourself for anything—whether it is under the name of reason or intelligence or feeling or conscience or some other lovely thing—that dominates or judges or controls the Word of God. It is not a matter of controlling it but of being controlled by it. The greatest of all God's servants are those who bow before that Word. Saint Paul, David, Luther, and Calvin were jealous to humble themselves in the dust before it, and if possible they would have gone still lower.

May it reign alone, this Word of my Savior God to which I am so delighted to be able to give this testimony again "before I depart and am no more" (Ps. 39:13). I give this testimony while waiting for the banner of eternal life (which we here on earth know how to open only half way) to be unfurled for us in the pure and serene light from above!

To read the talks in original
chronological order, go to
the next chapter.

ALL BY THE HOLY SPIRIT

(March 2, 1856)

"Now I am going to him who sent me, yet none of you asks me, 'Where are you going?' Because I have said these things, you are filled with grief. But I tell you the truth: It is for your good that I am going away. Unless I go away, the Counselor will not come to you; but if I go, I will send him to you. When he comes, he will convict the world of guilt in regard to sin and righteousness and judgment: in regard to sin, because men do not believe in me; in regard to righteousness, because I am going to the Father, where you can see me no longer; and in regard to judgment, because the prince of this world now stands condemned.

"I have much more to say to you, more than you can now bear. But when he, the Spirit of truth, comes, he will guide you into all truth. He will not speak on his own; he will speak only what he hears, and he will tell

you what is yet to come. He will bring glory to me by
taking from what is mine and making it known to you."

John 16:5–14

What a mercy it is, my beloveds, if we but knew how to
hear it, to receive this bread and this wine that the Savior
himself gives us saying, "This is my body, which is broken
for you; this is my blood, which is shed for you." Though absent, he is present with us, and more present being absent
than if he were here. Henceforth it is through close union
with the Lord, it is through the possession of his body and
his blood that we are called to do his work. It is in his
bruised body and his shed blood that we are called to suffer
all the anguish and pain of the flesh. As we are renewed by
the Holy Spirit in him who calls us to his eternal communion through the present, visible communion, we are enabled to do Jesus' work by receiving Jesus' strength, Jesus'
grace, and the divine nature in which we have been made
participants in Jesus through the promises of faith.[1]

Alas, we are people of little faith! What a sight we would
be to the world if we were people of great faith; of a faith like
that of the centurion, capable of arousing the admiration or
astonishment of the Lord himself; of a faith that, laying hold
of Jesus Christ, would lay hold in him of eternal life and of
all the treasures of grace that reside in this merciful Savior!

THE HOLY SPIRIT INTERPRETING SCRIPTURE

Some days ago, my dear friends, we considered the
thoughts in which a Christian rests when he arrives at that

1   See 2 Peter 1:4.

37

moment alluded to a while ago. Reaching the end of his career, he says to the Lord in his small measure, "I have finished the work which you have given me to do" (John 17:4 NKJV). (In any event, he says this if he has been faithful in his small measure.) In so doing, we were considering the power and truth of that Word through which the Lord has revealed himself to us and through which, day after day, he nourishes our souls. It thus becomes for us like a perpetual communion through which we live the life of Jesus Christ and carry out the work of Jesus Christ.

But let us not forget, and let us learn—whether from the statements of God's Word or from the humiliating experiences of life—that though that Word is all powerful and fully divine, causing Job to say, "Oh, how strong are the words of the LORD" (see Job 6:25), it has no power unless it is applied in our souls by that very Spirit who first caused it to be set down on the book's pages. This is the Spirit who worked in the hearts of Isaiah and Jeremiah, of Saint Paul and Saint John; the Spirit who chose them as his instruments and then guided them in order to give eternal truth to all human generations without risk of error. And it is this same Spirit who must rewrite that word in our hearts and fasten it there. Otherwise it is for us a dead word and without effect.

We could reread the Holy Scriptures for years without harvesting any real blessing, and we would be astonished to see it so weak and so little borne out by experience, if the Holy Spirit did not explain and apply the Word of God to us by coming to dwell within us. Now this same Spirit who applies and explains the Word of God to us is also the one who does everything else in us. The work of the Father who has freely saved us and the work of the Son who redeemed us by his blood both become vain without the work of the Holy

Spirit who opens our souls to believe in the Father and the Son and to live out these words of life.

The Battle for Our Hearts

Man, the heart of man, is presented to us in Scripture (where everything is grand, infinite, and eternal) as a theater that draws the attention of the holy angels and of the Lord himself. There a continual battle is being waged between the powers of hell and the powers of heaven; a battle that is nothing but the renewal of the great battle waged between these same forces in the internal and external life of our Lord Jesus Christ. In this battle he was made to be fully conqueror, and even we ourselves were in turn enabled to be more than conquerors in him who loved us. Thus we are either the slaves and agents of the spirit of darkness or the slaves, the blessed slaves and rich agents, of the Spirit of light and life. It is up to us to choose the one by unbelief or the other by faith, for it is written, "I have set before you today life and good, death and evil. . . . Therefore choose" (Deut. 30:15, 19 NKJV).

But there is a difference between these choices that is quite befitting the mercy of God. The spirit of Satan, no matter how ingenious he is at knocking on all the entrances and doors to our hearts, is still never able to unite himself completely with our spirits and to be one with them. The Spirit of God, on the other hand, deigns to penetrate inside of us and to unite himself so fully with us that we become temples of the Holy Spirit.

The Holy Spirit Dwelling Within Us

Being filled with the Spirit of Jesus Christ, we are enabled to do the works that he did and even, in a sense, to do greater works, as he himself said in announcing the promise of the Holy Spirit: "Anyone who has faith in me will do what I have been doing. He will do even greater things than these" (John 14:12). Jesus even tells his disciples that because of that Spirit from him—the Spirit for whom they are waiting—it is better for them that he go away. "It is for your good that I am going away" (John 16:7).

Oh, my Savior, how often I have longed to have you close to me the way Peter and John did, to be able to approach you, to converse with you, and to ask your advice! But behold, you yourself have told me that there is a gift so precious that, because of it, it is better for me that you go away; and you have given me this gift through the Holy Spirit.

Who among us understands and appreciates the gift of the Holy Spirit? All one can say is that God is granting to the faithful church of today the grace to sense how little it has appreciated and possessed that creative Spirit who is none other than God himself coming to dwell in us and make all things new there; that Spirit to whom nothing is impossible.

Blessed is the one who believes and does not doubt! If I have to conquer a formidable temptation, it is not I who must conquer. It is the Spirit of God in me called upon through prayer. If I have to bear unbearable pains of the flesh, it is not I who must bear them. It is the Spirit of God in me called upon through prayer. If I have to put on that spirit of love so contrary to our self-centered nature, it is not I who will exercise that power of love. It is the Spirit of God in me called upon through prayer. The same is true for everything else, so that in order to doubt that we could, through the Holy Spirit, accomplish the work to which we are called, we would have to start by doubting first that God is faithful in his promises and then that he has the power needed to accomplish them.

HONORING THE HOLY SPIRIT

Oh, my friends, said a dying Christian, even on our best days we have our eyes only half open, and I particularly apply that statement to the virtue and power of the Holy Spirit. If our eyes were fully open to see him and appreciate him, would there be so much trembling and complaining among us? Would we not always be seen as those who are filled with the power of Christ's fellowship for the accomplishing of our work?

My friends, see the place the Holy Spirit occupies in Scripture. See the place he occupies in the promises of the Old Testament, the place he occupies in the promises of Jesus Christ to his apostles, the transition he brings about between the Gospels and the Book of Acts, and the enormous change he produces in the apostles themselves. These things show to all the disciples of all ages what he is able to do at all times.

The Holy Spirit is the great promise of the New Testament; it is he who applies the crowning touch to all the rest. Elect of the Father, redeemed by the Son, it is only as we come to be filled with the Holy Spirit and to live his life that we gain possession of our inheritance. True, we are still waiting to harvest the fullness of that inheritance in a better world and under a more tranquil sky, freed from all the infirmities of the flesh and of the earth. Then we will no longer be anything except temples of the Holy Spirit so that even our bodies might be called glorious and spiritual bodies.

May this body of dust and sin soon fall to make room for that glorious body, that spiritual body in which we will ac-

41

complish the will of God with the perfection of Jesus Christ. Then we will know, by the light of the Holy Spirit, all the gifts of the Holy Spirit and all of his blessings. We will know them in order to enjoy them and, above all, that we might have learned to love as we have been loved!

To read the talks in original
chronological order, go to
the next chapter.

ALL IN JESUS CHRIST

(March 9, 1856)

When I came to you, brothers, I did not come with eloquence or superior wisdom as I proclaimed to you the testimony about God. For I resolved to know nothing while I was with you except Jesus Christ and him crucified. I came to you in weakness and fear, and with much trembling. My message and my preaching were not with wise and persuasive words, but with a demonstration of the Spirit's power, so that your faith might not rest on men's wisdom, but on God's power.

We do, however, speak a message of wisdom among the mature, but not the wisdom of this age or of the rulers of this age, who are coming to nothing. No, we speak of God's secret wisdom, a wisdom that has been hidden and that God destined for our glory before time began. None of the rulers of this age un-

derstood it, for if they had, they would not have crucified the Lord of glory. However, as it is written

"No eye has seen,
   no ear has heard,
no mind has conceived
   what God has prepared for those who love
      him"—

but God has revealed it to us by his Spirit.

1 Corinthians 2:1–10

In summing up with you, my dear friends, as before your
very eyes, the results in which I have been strengthened by
the experiences of life and of the gospel ministry and by the
study of the Word of God, I said last Sunday: All by the Holy
Spirit. Let us say today: All in Jesus Christ.

GOD IN CHRIST

We are sometimes led to think of Jesus as having only
opened the door to heaven for us and then having, in some
sense, abandoned us to get there on our own; but that is a
very narrow view of what the Lord has done and of what he
is for us. Saint Paul surely had something higher in mind
when he wrote, "For I resolved to know nothing while I was
with you except Jesus Christ and him crucified." For him,
the whole of God is summed up in Jesus Christ, and the
whole of Jesus Christ is summed up in his cross.

Elsewhere Paul says, "Christ Jesus . . . has become for us
wisdom from God—that is, our righteousness, holiness and
redemption" (1 Cor. 1:30). Here we see that Jesus Christ

44

was not given to us simply to blot out our sins through his once shed blood, but he was given to us again, having been reconciled with God by that precious blood, in order to guide us, to sanctify us, to fill us with wisdom, and to accomplish all in all. Again Paul says, "For in Christ all the fullness of the Deity lives in bodily form" (Col. 2:9). It is in the flesh, in a visible form that God dwells in Christ, but all of him dwells there, with all of his glory and all of his eternal perfections.

And still elsewhere, another very profound passage by the same author says, "All things are yours, . . . and you are of Christ, and Christ is of God" (1 Cor. 3:21, 23). Here we see God, through a wonderful, marvelous hierarchy, at the head of the entire order of eternal truth, sending and directing his Son. We see his Son in turn calling us and adopting us to himself, so that in the name of this Son we might have dominion over all things and so that we might possess the entire universe through being members of him to whom the entire universe is submitted. "All things are yours," first level; "and you are of Christ," second level; "and Christ is of God," first, or rather, third level, the supreme level to which everything else is attached and upon which everything else depends.

ETERNAL LIFE IN CHRIST

We are now quite far from the thinking of those who regard Jesus Christ as having simply accomplished an act, the principal act of salvation! Jesus Christ is the God of man, as Pascal said so well in a few pages where he develops in a deeply Christian way Jesus Christ's place between God and us. He is the God of man. He is God who has given himself to us, and he has given himself completely. When we possess Jesus Christ by a true faith, we possess nothing less than God himself, and in him eternal life. "He who has the Son has life; . . . God has given us eternal life, and this life is in his Son" (1 John 5:12, 11).

OUR NEEDS MET IN CHRIST

In addition, whatever the need to be satisfied in our souls and in our entire existence, earthly and eternal, we find it in Jesus Christ.

Is our need first of all the blotting out of our sins? He has blotted them out by his blood. There is only one thing in the world that blots out sins. It is not our acts of contrition, not our repentance, not our alms or our good works. It is not even our prayers. It is the blood of Jesus Christ: "the blood of Jesus Christ . . . cleanses us from all sin" (1 John 1:7 NKJV). All sin that the blood of Jesus Christ has covered is forever annihilated before God. God no longer sees it, and I could use even stronger language without straying from Scripture. "God himself seeks them," says a prophet, "and no longer finds them" (see Jer. 50:20). He has put our "sins behind his back" (Isa. 38:17) so as not to look upon them any more. He will "hurl all our iniquities into the depths of the sea" (Micah 7:19), and in beholding us in Christ, he beholds us without sin, just like Christ himself, who was made "to be sin for us, so that in him we might become the righteousness of God" (2 Cor. 5:21).

Is it a matter of being consoled in our troubles? We go to Jesus Christ, who has suffered as we have, more than we have, infinitely more than we could suffer, infinitely more than we could conceive of suffering. All of our pain and sorrow is nothing but a tiny brook removed from the river of his infinite pain. In the same way, it is from his cross that all consolation and all mercy flow. It is to the Man of Sorrows that we go to seek consolation and peace, knowing that he is well acquainted with weariness and that by approaching him we will not only find the easing of our pains, but we will even see real blessing in them. Thus our bitterest afflictions will be found, in the end, to be his most remarkable mercies.

Is it a matter of light and of wisdom, of strength and of resisting sin? Is it a matter of this world or of the other? All is in Christ. Having Christ we have all things, but deprived of him we have absolutely nothing. That is why the apostle Saint Paul says in that marvelous passage that I just quoted, "All things are yours, and you are of Christ, and Christ is of God." All things are yours if you are of Christ, who is of God. It is not the relationship of God to Christ that will be contested by anyone. It is not the relationship of Christ to us that can be questioned if we are true Christians. So then, what is the result? That all things are ours.

Am I poor? All of the fortunes of this world are mine because they belong to Christ, who belongs to God. He would certainly know how to give to me, with him and in addition to him, all the fortunes of the world if they would be useful to me. If, in place of riches, he gives me poverty, it is because this is better for me and the result of God's choice. The entire world with all its glory and power belongs to me because they belong to my Father, who will give them to me tomorrow and who could give them to me today if that were good, because he dispenses them according to his pleasure.

Am I sick? Health is mine, strength is mine, well-being is mine, a perfect enjoyment of all the good things of life is mine, because all that is Christ's, who is God's and who dispenses them according to his pleasure. And to whom would he dispense them if not to me, his child? If then he refuses them to me today, for a fleeting moment that passes like a ship of the mist, he has his reasons. It is because there are in these pains and this bitterness hidden blessings that are worth more to me than that health which is so precious or that well-being which is so sweet. He will never deprive me of any good except to give me some other, better one. That is my consolation; it is all in his love.

Is it a question of wisdom and light? Well then, even if I were ignorant all my life, if I never had the opportunity to cultivate my worldly abilities, I am still wise in Christ. Knowing Christ, I am wiser and more enlightened about the things of God than the man of this world who has spent a lifetime growing pale over his books, for I know that uncreated, eternal light that he doesn't know. This is the light in which God himself rejoices and by which I am unfailingly led through all the dark places of life.

I defy you to find anything of which I could not say, "That belongs to my Father; therefore it is mine. If he refuses it to me today, he will give it to me tomorrow. I entrust myself to his love. All is mine if I am Christ's."

OUR GRATITUDE FOR CHRIST CRUCIFIED

Also note that Saint Paul says in the chapter we read at the outset, "I resolved to know nothing while I was with you except Jesus Christ and him crucified." Oh, my friends, let us not be so ungrateful as to forget that it is beneath the cross and through the cross that Jesus Christ purchased us and earned that enormous bliss that I am trying to describe and that I fail even to glimpse or imagine. It is by his shed

blood, it is by his unimaginable sufferings that he has accomplished everything for us. His love is the source of our
full deliverance and redemption—such is the Savior. Thus
we have begun, and it is thus that we must end. We come to
his cross, we sit down beneath his cross, we desire only that
nothing in this world will uproot us from that place. We desire to live there, and we desire to die there.

Dear friends, soon the scenes of this world will have
passed away. We have anguish in the world, but be of good
courage, Jesus Christ has overcome the world. The strong
man has been bound by one stronger than he. And now here
we are in the presence of Christ, who has redeemed us with
his blood and who waits for us in order to fill us with glory
and bliss.

Do you not desire his glory? Do you not desire his love?
Know him such as he is. Embrace him completely by a sincere faith, so that you might experience those admirable
words of the apostle on which we have just meditated. That
is how you might be happy in life and happier still in death.
That is how this life, which is so sad for the man of the
world, might be for you an existence whose light and peace
will be ever increasing until the day of Christ. To him be
given the praise, honor, and glory, and, above all, the
homage of our hearts along with a love corresponding, if
possible, to his own!

To read the talks in original
chronological order, go to
the next chapter.

BLESSED TRINITY

(March 16, 1856)

Therefore, brethren, we are debtors—not to the flesh, to live according to the flesh. For if you live according to the flesh, you will die; but if by the Spirit you put to death the deeds of the body, you will live. For as many as are led by the Spirit of God, these are sons of God. For you did not receive the spirit of bondage again to fear, but you received the Spirit of adoption, by whom we cry out, "Abba, Father." The Spirit himself bears witness with our spirit that we are children of God, and if children, then heirs—heirs of God and joint heirs with Christ, if indeed we suffer with him, that we may also be glorified together.

Romans 8:12–17 NKJV

Holy Scripture is wise even in its silence. You would search there in vain for the word *trinity* to express the doctrine on which, if God lends me the strength, I have it on my heart to say a few words. Why? Because that word *trinity* presents to our spirits the idea of something speculative, while the doctrine that was much later named—and quite well named—by human theology "the Trinity" is the most practical and tender thing in the world. It is the very expression of the love that is in God, be it in his relationships with humanity or in the internal relationships of the Godhead. The root of our salvation is in the love of God. "We love because he first loved us" (1 John 4:19). "God is love" (1 John 4:8, 16), and that love is demonstrated to us in the work of our salvation. Yet it reveals itself not only as saving us, but also as existing through all eternity in the bosom of God, working his eternal bliss before accomplishing ours and that of all his faithful creatures.

When someone wants to take account of how the love of God operates toward his poor lost creatures in order to give them the eternal life that they lost through their works, he has only quite simply to follow the historical order in which God has given us his revelations and inspired the Scriptures to his apostles after having done so to his prophets. It is thus that we find first the God of the Old Testament, then the God of the Gospels, and then the God of the Epistles and of gospel prophecy.

GOD FOR US

In the Old Testament, we learn already that which should suffice to fill our hearts with joy. . . . We learn that even though we have rendered ourselves unworthy of his love, God loves us anyhow. We would have merited a thousand times that he declare himself to be against us, and if someone is not pierced by that thought, he has only to reread the prophets, Ezekiel in particular. They are filled with that terrible doctrine of the judgments of God that the Israelites drew upon themselves by their evil works—even though they did not merit those judgments any more than the rest of humanity, whose history is mirrored in that of Israel. But behold that instead of declaring himself to be against us, God declares that he is for us. We learn that where we should expect to find only a treasure of wrath, we find instead a treasure of mercy.

The omnipotent God who created heaven and earth, the author of the visible world and of the invisible world, is *for us* completely. He asks only to save us. Whoever wants to enter into God's thoughts, to confess his sins, and to submit to God's grace will possess eternal life just as if he had never sinned. Or rather, he will possess it having sinned but having been reconciled. He will possess it with a new sense of the mercy that is in God.

It is thus that God reveals himself to us in the Old Testament and thus that, lifting this heavy burden of divine wrath, divine love bursts out everywhere. These same prophets who proclaim such terrible judgments cannot for long sustain such language. They always finish with words of mercy. You will find this in a very remarkable way in the prophet Micah, who, in the briefness of his pages, develops with admirable fullness the plan of condemnation, of prophecy, and of the salvation in which he ends up resting.

GOD WITH US

Then come the Gospels, which were predicted by the prophets. There God takes one more step: he approaches us.

He does not rest content to tell us from afar that he is for us, but he comes quite near to live *with us* as one of us—Son of man, taken from among men, while he is still fully Son of God. After having been for us, he is with us, very close to us as a friend and a brother; one with whom, according to the expression of Psalm 55, we can "share all of our secrets."[1] Thus God shows himself to us in an even more tender and reassuring way than we have seen in the Old Testament, especially when that friend and brother finishes revealing to us the doctrine of divine justice and divine mercy by dying for us on the cross, blotting out our sins.

But, while such a tender relationship is unfolded from God to us, another relationship is unfolded within the bosom of God. We learn that the one who redeems us is the Son of the one who wants to save us. We learn that there is between God such as he is revealed in the Old Testament and God as he appears in the Gospels the touching relationship of a father to his son. This is a relationship that we cannot fathom to its depths in God but that we can at least discern to be something inexpressibly tender and yet, at the same time, mysterious.

Note well that one of these relationships could not work without the other. We will never understand what God is for us in Jesus Christ if we do not glimpse what Jesus Christ is for God, especially since there is something here that must not escape us. We only understand the spirit of love in its fullness as the spirit of sacrifice. Yet it would seem that there can be no sacrifice in God, for what could take away from one moment of his eternal bliss? But see how in the person

---

1 The specific reference in Psalm 55 is not clear. Psalm 44:21, however, reminds us that God already "knows the secrets of the heart."

of his Son, the Lord of lords gives us the example of sacrifice. See how the one who is the Son of the Father is at the same time the "man of sorrows." See how the inexpressible enormity of the suffering of which humanity is capable (but only capable within that union with divinity) unfolds before our touched and grateful gaze in the one in whom "all the fullness of the Deity lives in bodily form" (Col. 2:9). And do you not see that this very moving doctrine disappears completely if the Son is not one with the Father? Do you not see that what excites our tender gratitude for the Lord Jesus Christ is tied to the fact that he is truly the Son of God, which is to say God, just as he is the Son of man, which is to say man?

GOD IN US

Now come the Epistles and gospel prophecy. How do they open? With the descent of the Holy Spirit, who establishes the church as he is poured out upon it. This is the third and last step that God takes toward his poor, fallen creatures, for we could not conceive of another. He was with us, and behold, he comes to establish himself *in us.* He comes to make himself so thoroughly one with us that out of these poor bodies born of dust and become slaves of sin he forms temples of his Spirit, the dwelling place of God where he is pleased to rest. The Holy Spirit, that is to say, God, comes to give himself to us after having been for us in the Old Testament and with us in the Gospels. This is the last overflowing measure of divine love that could not be content without being made one with us and coming to dwell in us: "he in us, and we in him" (see John 14:20).

Here again, my dear friends, note that all the power of

this doctrine of life disappears if the Holy Spirit, instead of being God, was only something sent from God, an action of God, a gift of God. This would only bring us back to what we know abundantly from the Old Testament and from the Gospels of the power and grace that God can and desires to communicate to us. By contrast, the Holy Spirit as he is revealed to us in the Epistles, in the end of the New Testament, and in the promises of Jesus Christ to his disciples, is truly God. He is the power of God, which strengthens us; the peace of God, which comforts us; the holiness of God, which frees us from evil; and the life of God, which causes our hearts to beat.

Oh, who could measure and understand the enormity of the progress between the last chapter of the Gospels and the first chapter of Acts? Who could account for this admirable sequence of divine revelation and gifts in the three parts of Holy Scripture that we have just run through (alas, so rapidly given the subject while at too great length given the small strength of the speaker)? Admirable perspective, which I can only outline.

GOD IN THREE PERSONS

The relationship of the Father, of the Son, and of the Holy Spirit to man corresponds to a relationship of the Father, of the Son, and of the Holy Spirit in God, and the love that is poured out to save us is the expression of the love that dwells eternally in the heart of God. Ah, how moving and profound this makes the doctrine we are pondering! In it is the foundation of the gospel, and those who reject it as a speculative and purely theological doctrine have therefore never understood the first thing about it. It is the strength of our hearts, the joy of our souls, the life of our lives, and the very basis of revealed truth.

I am obliged to stop and leave to your meditations the things that I would have liked to add. In finishing, I must content myself with recalling to you a saying that I have often cited from the pulpit but that some of those here have perhaps not heard. It sums up admirably the whole of this doctrine. A father of the church said, "We have in the Old Testament *God for us,* in the Gospels *God with us,* and in Acts and the Epistles *God in us.*" It is this God for you, with you, and in you; it is the Father, Son, and Holy Spirit that I desire for you as for myself, in life and in death, from the depths of a heart that is devoted to you in Jesus Christ!

To read the talks in original
chronological order, go to
chapt. 24 on page 171.

part 3
Living
Our Faith

Take my life and let it be
Consecrated, Lord, to thee;
Take my moments and my days,
Let them flow in ceaseless praise, Let them flow in
ceaseless praise.

Take my will and make it thine,
It shall be no longer mine;
Take my heart, it is thine own,
It shall be thy royal throne, It shall be thy royal
throne.

Take my love; my Lord, I pour
At thy feet its treasure store.
Take myself and I will be
Ever, only, all for thee, Ever, only, all for thee.
Frances Ridley Havergal
1836–1879

This section contains a number of Adolphe Monod's practical teachings, which can strengthen our faith as they motivate and equip us to live more consistent Christian lives.

57

Two Great Goods

(October 21, 1855)

For I know that through your prayers and the help given by the Spirit of Jesus Christ, what has happened to me will turn out for my deliverance. I eagerly expect and hope that I will in no way be ashamed, but will have sufficient courage so that now as always Christ will be exalted in my body, whether by life or by death. For to me, to live is Christ and to die is gain. If I am to go on living in the body, this will mean fruitful labor for me. Yet what shall I choose? I am torn between the two: I desire to depart and be with Christ, which is better by far; but it is more necessary for you that I remain in the body. Convinced of this, <u>I know that I will remain, and I will continue with all of you for your progress and joy in the faith,</u> so that through my being with you again your joy in Christ Jesus will overflow on account of me.

Philippians 1:19–26

My dear friends, I would like to draw your attention to the attitude in which the holy apostle here considers life and death. First of all, note the statement that serves as his point of departure and that is like the motto of his Christian life: "For to me, to live is Christ and to die is gain." "To live is Christ," that is to say, my life, my natural life, which I live today and to which I may die tomorrow, is used for nothing but to follow and to serve Jesus Christ. "To die is gain." That statement needs no explanation.

Continuing on, the apostle asks himself which is worth more to him, to live or to die. That question often presents itself to us, and perhaps we have answered like the apostle. It is to be feared, however, that it was said with a very different sentiment. When we have desired death it meant: I don't know which I dread more, the afflictions of life, from which death would deliver me, or the terrors of death, from which life preserves me. That is to say that life and death seem to us like two evils, the lesser of which we cannot discern. As for the apostle, they appear to him as two enormous goods, the greater of which he cannot discern. Personally, he prefers to die in order to be with Christ. Concerning the church and the world, he prefers to live in order to serve Christ, to extend his reign, and to gain souls for him. What an admirable view of life and death; admirable because it is completely dominated, completely sanctified by love and is like the view that Jesus Christ himself had. Let us devote ourselves to entering into this sentiment.

RECOGNIZING THEM AS GOOD

Life is good; death is good. Death is good because it frees us from the miseries of this life and above all because, even if life for us were filled with all the joys that earth can give, death causes us to enter into a joy and a glory that we cannot even begin to imagine. We must therefore consider death as something desirable in itself. Let us not distance ourselves from that which reminds us of it. Let all of the diseases, all of the deaths suffered, everything that goes on around us remind us that for each one of us it can come at any moment.

Life is also good because we can serve Jesus Christ, glorify Jesus Christ, imitate Jesus Christ. It is not worth living for anything else. All that we have of strength, of breath, of life, of resources must be consecrated, devoted, sanctified, crucified for the service of our Lord Jesus Christ. This crucified life is the blessed life, even in the midst of earth's bitterest pains. It is a life in which we can taste and pour out around us the most precious blessings. Let us love life, let us sense the price of life, but only in order to fill it with Jesus Christ. For us to have such an attitude requires the Holy Spirit transforming us into new men.

But let us be careful to note that it is not just a matter of having our spirits sustained, comforted, strengthened. The Spirit of God must come to dwell within us. Often we make a real effort to work on ourselves, to keep watch over our own spirit. That is good, but it is not sufficient. We need more. We need to have Jesus Christ himself living in our hearts by his Holy Spirit.

Enjoying Them

Oh, my friends! Let us consider the promises of the gospel, and we will see how far we are from possessing and enjoying them. May God be willing to open heaven above our heads, reveal all things to us, fill us with all wisdom, and cause us to see that even here on earth we can attain to perfect joy while waiting to possess fullness of bliss and victory. May he cause us to gather in the blessings that heaven is pleased to pour out on an earth that opens to receive them. May it thus be made known that if earth is able to beat us down and trouble us, it cannot extinguish the heavenly virtues, annihilate the promises of God, or throw a veil, not even the lightest mist, over the love with which God has loved us in Jesus Christ!

To read the talks in original
chronological order, go to
the next chapter.

COMMUNION WITH
CHRIST

(October 28, 1855)

For I received from the Lord what I also passed on to you: The Lord Jesus, on the night he was betrayed, took bread, and when he had given thanks, he broke it and said, "This is my body, which is for you; do this in remembrance of me." In the same way, after supper he took the cup, saying, "This cup is the new covenant in my blood; do this, whenever you drink it, in remembrance of me." For whenever you eat this bread and drink this cup, you proclaim the Lord's death until he comes.

1 Corinthians 11:23–26

My dear friends, I want you to know that in taking communion frequently during my illness I am finding much sweetness and, I hope, also much fruit. It is a great ill that communion is so rarely celebrated in our church,[1] and an ill that much effort is being made from all sides to remedy. Our reformers, in establishing this order of things, were careful to explain that they were doing it only for a time and only in order to prevent the very serious abuses that had slipped into the primitive church. But that which they established for a time has persisted through the centuries in the majority of our churches. Now, at last, we are coming to a time when frequent communion will be restored to us.

BENEFITS OF FREQUENT COMMUNION

Calvin said somewhere that communion should be celebrated at least every Sunday. Note that "at least." If every Sunday is *at least,* what then is *at most?* According to Calvin (and this refers rather clearly to the Book of Acts) at most is to take it as the first Christians took it: to take it every day, from house to house following the family meal.

Each of you has been able to note that infrequent communion leads to some strange and extraordinary ideas about this sacrament, about the preparation that must precede it, and about the feelings that follow it. There is reason to believe that it is this rareness of communion that has given rise to the majority of controversies raised on the subject.

On the contrary, frequent communion leads to a much better understanding of the true character of this sacrament, and it is impossible that daily communion would not cause this character to be clearly grasped. It teaches us to relate communion to everything that is most natural in the Christian life, just as eating is the most natural thing in ordinary

1 The Reformed Church of France.

life. In any event, it is in seeing in communion the simplest expression of our faith that we will profit the most from it, that we will draw the most fruit from it, and that it will nourish our souls with the flesh and blood of Jesus Christ.

UNDERSTANDING COMMUNION

In our confession of faith there are several statements on this subject that are so beautiful that I would like you to hear them. They express just what I would like to tell you myself.

We confess that the Lord's Supper . . . is a witness of the union which we have with Christ, inasmuch as he not only died and rose again for us once, but also feeds and nourishes us truly with his flesh and blood, so that we may be one in him, and that our life may be in common. Although he be in heaven until he come to judge all the earth, still we believe that by the secret and incomprehensible power of his Spirit he feeds and strengthens us with the substance of his body and of his blood. We hold that this is done spiritually, not because we put imagination and fancy in the place of fact and truth, but because the greatness of this mystery exceeds the measure of our senses and the laws of nature. . . .

We believe . . . that in the Lord's Supper, as well as in baptism, God gives us really and in fact that which he there sets forth to us; and that consequently with these signs is given the true possession and enjoyment of that which they present to us. And thus all who bring a pure faith, like a vessel, to the sacred table of Christ, receive truly that of which it is a sign; for the body and the blood of Jesus Christ give food and drink to the soul, no less than bread and wine nourish the body.

. . . [T]he bread and wine given to us in the sacrament serve to our spiritual nourishment, inasmuch as they show, as to our sight, that the body of Christ is our meat, and his blood our drink.[2]

To this admirable quotation I would only add that after Pastor Verney read it one day to several Lutheran friends who were discussing communion with him, his friends said, "That is the exact expression of our faith," to which Mr. Verney replied that these words were taken from the confession of faith of the reformed churches. This proves that by holding strictly to Scripture, as is done here, faith and love prevail in the field of controversy.[3]

LOOKING BEYOND THE ELEMENTS

Very well, my friends, that to which we bear witness through the communion we have just celebrated is that the

---

2 This English quotation from the 1559 French Confession of Faith (also known as the Confession of La Rochelle) is taken from volume 3 of Philip Schaff's *The Creeds of Christendom,* 6th ed., 3 vols. (Grand Rapids, Mich.: Baker, 1996, reprinted by arrangement with Harper and Row), 380–81.

3 It is interesting to note, in this context, that the Sunday Gatherings at which these exhortations were given were the occasion for Monod and his listeners to take communion together each week (Calvin's "at least" frequency). These were also ecumenical gatherings, with pastors from the Reformed, Lutheran, Wesleyan, and evangelical churches taking turns presiding at the Lord's Table.

Savior's flesh and blood are "real food" and "real drink" (John 6:55). We bear witness that the entire Christian ambition of our souls is to nourish ourselves on them day and night and to seek all of our strength in a true, deep, living communion with Jesus Christ, in all his fullness.

It is by prayer that we maintain ourselves in that communion with Jesus Christ that will enable us to do what he did and to be what he was. It is by the prayer of faith. It is by persevering, ardent prayer that accepts no denial, that wants to enjoy all that the Father has promised us in his Word, and that is never silent. It is by prayer that continues on its knees and that pursues its task in spite of blood and tears *until* it has obtained what it asks for.

Oh, how great our strength would be, how great our joy would be, unchangeable and independent of all the sufferings of this miserable body. This body is perhaps half torn and destroyed, but it is henceforth the temple of the Holy Spirit and will tomorrow be transformed into a glorious spiritual body—that is to say, completely filled with the Holy Spirit like Jesus Christ's own body. How great our joy would be, not if we had the means (for we have them), but if we utilized the means that we have to conquer the pains and struggles of the flesh so as always to arrive at the heart of our Father, the joy of our Savior, and the power of the Holy Spirit.

The Role of the Holy Spirit in Communion

Meditate, I beseech you, on the Holy Spirit. Read and reread Jesus Christ's discourses in the last chapters of Saint John. Read the eighth chapter of Romans and other similar passages in order to learn what resources of strength and of comfort we have in the Holy Spirit, who is no less than God himself. Yes, my God, no less than you, yourself, coming to inhabit the body of your poor child; sinful, miserable, destroyed by suffering and sin but saved by grace and washed in the blood of the spotless Lamb! Why, when we have such promises, would we let ourselves stop half way? Why would we groan in our hunger and our thirst when we have before us an abundantly laden table, toward which we need only extend the hand of faith in order to feed ourselves until we are fully satisfied and have life in abundance?

Ah! If only the small handful of Christians who are here could fully make up their minds to be truly happy, to pray "praying"[4] like Elijah. If only they could make up their minds to overcome their natural cowardice, their spiritual laziness, their unbelief! What could we not accomplish if we were to go off through the world like the twelve apostles? We would stir up all Paris. We would win over all our brothers and sisters, who would be moved by seeing the gospel lived out in our lives.

PRAYER

My God, here is our deepest misery, that having such promises we should do so little. Come help us! and grant that this small communion of the upper room might be the seed of a new Christian life for all those who partook of it or were present here. May we thus be enabled to live and die and be made so conformable to Jesus Christ that we might

---

4 This is taken from a more literal rendering of the Greek in James 5:17, which is usually translated "he prayed earnestly."

live as he lived; that just as he said, "Anyone who has seen me has seen the Father" (John 14:9), so we might be able to say, "Anyone who has seen me has seen my Master." Pour out this blessing on these friends who have come to console me in my affliction, my blessed affliction.

To read the talks in original
chronological order, go to
chapt. 15 on page 99.

SCRIPTURE'S REWARDS

(November 11, 1855)

For you have been born again not of seed which is perishable but imperishable, that is, through the living and abiding word of God. For,

"All flesh is like grass,
And all its glory like the flowers of grass;
The grass withers,
And the flower falls off,
But the word of the Lord abides forever."

And this is the word that was preached to you.

Therefore, putting aside all malice and all guile and hypocrisy and envy and all slander, like newborn babies, long for the pure milk of the word, that by it you may grow in respect to salvation, if you have tasted the kindness of the Lord.

1 Peter 1:23–2:3 NASB

It is my custom on these occasions to address a few words of Christian exhortation to the few friends who are kind enough to gather around me. Today my state of suffering forbids me that consolation, so I must content myself with giving you an example from Christian experience that will be able to lead you into healthy reflection on the value of the Word of God. I take this example, in all simplicity, from what happened to me this past week.

A NIGHT WELL SPENT

During one of those nights in which I suffered much and slept little, toward morning, at around 4:30 a.m., I had settled myself in my bed with the hope of getting a little rest. Then I invited the person keeping watch over me—one of those fine young men who have the goodness to devote part of their strength to me[1]—to read me a chapter from God's Word. He offered to read me the eighth chapter of the Epistle to the Romans. I accepted while asking him to go back to the sixth and even the fifth chapters so as to follow the development of the ideas.

After we had read chapters 5, 6, 7, and 8 in order, my attention, my interest, and my admiration had been so stirred by the heavenly language of Saint Paul—or rather of the Holy Spirit speaking through Saint Paul—that I no longer dreamed of sleep. So we read the ninth chapter and the fol-

1 This small group of young friends, almost all of whom were medical students, watched over Adolphe Monod each night for over six months, easing his long hours of sleeplessness and suffering through their devotion and affectionate care. (Footnote taken from *Les Adieux*, 21st ed. [Annemass, Haute-Savoie, France: Editions des Groupes Missionaries, 1978].)

71

lowing ones, right to the end, always with the same sustained interest. Finally, we read the first four chapters in order to have left nothing out and to have read the entire epistle.

The reading had taken about two hours, and I no longer dreamed of anything except hearing the Word of God and profiting from it. The Lord in his goodness had provided for the rest that I had been missing.

HARVESTING SCRIPTURE'S REWARDS

I don't know how to communicate to you how much I was struck in that reading of the entire Epistle to the Romans with that mark of divinity, of truth, of holiness, of love, and of power that is imprinted on every page and on every word. We sensed, my young friend and I, without at first communicating our thoughts, that we were listening to a voice from heaven. We sensed that, independent of all those testimonies that witness to the inspiration and divine authority of Scripture, it provides a completely sufficient testimony to itself, just as Jesus Christ did to himself through his works.

We also sensed how useful it is to read Scripture as a whole and how much one loses in taking only portions, fragments, detached verses. A book is understood only when, from time to time, it is read as a whole. This led us to understand that one needs to make two studies of the Word of God: a comprehensive one to produce in us the very blessed impression that we had just received, and a detailed one to let each verse and each word be taken into account.

But our principal impression was one of humiliation. We said to one another, "What! We have such a treasure as this near us, and we fail to draw on it!" We had just spent two hours in heaven. We found ourselves transported not only into the midst of the best among men—those instruments who were inspired and favored by the Holy Spirit—but also into the midst of the elect angels and into the company of Jesus Christ.

We have resolved, while relying on the only one who can guard his children's resolutions, to give ourselves over with renewed zeal to the study of Scripture, sacrificing, if need be, a myriad of other readings that are instructive and useful but that cannot compare with the Word of God. We have resolved to live with that Word as we desire to live with God himself, because reading that Word inspired by God's Spirit is like a conversation with God.

I commend to you, my dear friends, the Word of God as something for constant, in-depth study and meditation. It will lift us up above everything else. It will, through Jesus Christ, be the strength of our lives, the joy of our hearts, and our powerful consolation in life and in death. I ask it for you as for myself.

To read the talks in original
chronological order, go to
the next chapter.

THE PRIVILEGE OF GLORIFYING GOD

(November 18, 1855)

Whether you eat or drink or whatever you do, do it all for the glory of God.

1 Corinthians 10:31

Our brother's prayer that we just heard was filled with the thought that we must, each one of us, according to his position, glorify God. I would like, in a few words, to make you sense and to make myself sense what an immense privilege it is to be called to glorify God.

GOD'S INVITATION

Think of it! God, the sovereign Creator, the unique Author of all things, through whose will alone they subsist and have been created; God, the only Savior of lost and guilty humanity, the only Comforter of suffering humanity; God, from whom proceeds every good thing, who has absolutely no need of us; God invites us to add something to his glory by bearing witness to him before his creatures, thus contributing our share to the sanctification of his name. He wants this to be the supreme law of our lives.

True piety, just like true wisdom and true philosophy (even of the human variety), requires that there be a unique guiding principle that directs our entire lives and to which everything else relates. And that unity that men go searching after, some in the world and others within themselves or in an imaginary God, we find in the living and true God, who alone is holy, alone is wise, alone is eternal. On him alone depend both our unfolding eternal happiness and the smallest sense of well-being that we can savor from day to day in the stirrings of our hearts or even in the sensations of our poor bodies.

Who are those whom he calls to contribute to his glory? It is the angels, and they are quite blessed to do so. They are aware of what a great privilege it is for them. But it is not only the angels. It is also us, miserable sinners, worthy of the wrath of God, placed under his curse by our works. God does not content himself with drawing us by the hand out of this deep pit. Even as he is drawing us out he says to us, "Now glorify me," as if we could give something back to the one from whom we have received everything, beginning with the forgiveness of our sins.

OUR ACCEPTANCE

Ah, if we could only sense what grace God shows us in using us to add something to his glory, we would not be busy with anything else, and we would, my beloveds, find in it the sweetest and deepest consolation we could ever taste. For it is not only pardoned sinners who are called thus to glorify God after having been saved. It is also sinners who are hurting, miserable, and dragging painfully through life with sufferings of soul and body. These would seem to be excluded from the privilege of glorifying God, absorbed as they are by the sorrows and pains of this life. Ah, but not at all! These are the ones who are especially called to glorify him and who find in their sufferings, as they found in their cancelled sins, one more way to give glory to the one who has taught us to say, "When I am weak, then I am strong" (2 Cor. 12:10).

What a consolation for those who suffer to be able to say to themselves, "Through my sufferings, which I endure patiently and peacefully while waiting to do so joyfully and gloriously, I can give to God a glory that I would not otherwise have been able to give him." Oh, what infinite sweetness those who suffer find in that thought! It is thus, above all, that suffering is a privilege. For a Christian, to suffer is a privilege; to suffer much is a special privilege. All those who suffer should enter into my thought and "commit their souls to him in doing good, as to a faithful Creator" (1 Pet. 4:19 NKJV).

Alas, we cannot do it ourselves. "The spirit indeed is willing, but the flesh is weak" (Mark 14:38 NKJV), and the moment after we have lifted ourselves up into heaven by the simple words of the gospel, there is that miserable flesh that encumbers us and that, so to speak, takes us by the feet, drags us to earth, and chains us there with the weight of pain. My friends, this is the struggle of our entire life. It is the struggle of life; it is the struggle of death.

But we have Jesus with us, the author and perfecter of our faith, who was himself consecrated through suffering and who is therefore also powerful to sustain those who are tempted. Let our constant prayer be, "Lord, increase our faith!" (Luke 17:5 KJV); "I do believe; help me overcome my unbelief" (Mark 9:24).

Oh, my friends, who have come in brotherly love to unite with me in celebrating this sweet communion that is for us such a living picture of our communion with God and with one another, may God bless each one of you, and may he give each of us the grace to live only for his glory, to suffer only for his glory, to speak only for his glory, while waiting that we might die for his glory, in Jesus Christ crucified and resurrected!

PRAYER

Oh, my God, pour out on each one of us with infinite generosity all of the blessings that you hold in Jesus Christ. Grant us the grace to live in fellowship with you and to glorify you so that your will might be done on this poor earth as it is in heaven, through Jesus Christ our Lord. Look with compassion on this world for which Jesus Christ died and which is still plunged in darkness, in disaster, in filth, and in crime. Look with compassion on your church, which you have chosen in the world and which has turned aside from your holy designs, having taken on the likeness of the world while preserving the name of church. Look upon us and upon all of your children. Look upon all those who suffer. We place under your protection the numerous and touching family of the afflicted, the sick, the prisoners, the slaves, the persecuted (especially those persecuted for righteousness), and the oppressed of every kind. Teach them to turn eyes of faith toward you. Hasten the spread of the reign of Jesus Christ. May it come, and may what you have done in sending him into the world be recognized! Amen.

To read the talks in original
chronological order, go to
the next chapter.

DEMONSTRATING GOD'S LOVE

(November 25, 1855)

A new command I give you: Love one another. As I have loved you, so you must love one another. By this all men will know that you are my disciples, if you love one another. . . .

As the Father has loved me, so have I loved you. Now remain in my love. If you obey my commands, you will remain in my love, just as I have obeyed my Father's commands and remain in his love. I have told you this so that my joy may be in you and that your joy may be complete. My command is this: Love each other as I have loved you. Greater love has no one than this, that he lay down his life for his friends.

John 13:34–35; 15:9–13

I was afraid, dear friends, that being overcome by suffering and fatigue I would be unable to speak these few words to you today. Yet the Lord has once again granted me grace by giving me some measure of relief. Please understand how grateful I am for the ability he leaves me, contrary to all human expectation, to exercise in some small measure each Sunday this ministry that I would like to continue exercising right up to the last breath of my life. My ministry is my life, and I feel that when I shall have no further ministry to exercise, I will be gathered up to exercise a different and better one. Please ask God not to withdraw from me this consolation of being able to receive each Sunday the body and blood of my Savior, which strengthens my body and soul in him, and also to speak a few words of edification and exhortation to my brothers.

GOD IS LOVE

Last Sunday I stressed briefly with those friends who were here (and who change each week) the immense privilege it is to be able to glorify God; something we are not only permitted but commanded to do. Today I will add that there is one way in which we are especially required and especially blessed to be able to glorify him. If, among the perfections of God that we are called to exhibit before men, there were one perfection whose manisfestation gave him special pleasure, would we not best give glory to him by imitating and demonstrating that perfection in ourselves? Very well then, what is the perfection through which God best manifests his presence? Is it not goodness?

Is it not written, "God is love"? God is righteous, and yet it is not written, "God is righteousness." God is powerful, and yet it is not written, "God is power." But there are two perfections to which that singular honor is given by the beloved disciple leaning on his Savior's bosom: holiness and love. "God is light. God is love."[1] And while he says once in his first epistle, "God is light" (1 John 1:5), he says twice in the space of a few verses, "God is love" (1 John 4:8, 16), as if to lift this perfection even higher than the other. If this is so, my dear friends, what we need to do to glorify God is to manifest that love that is in him in such a way that in seeing us live, in hearing us speak, in observing us act, in watching us suffer and live and die, someone would be able not to admire us but to admire the love of God in us.

LOVE IN ACTION

How can we manifest the love of God? Jesus Christ showed us how. He demonstrated God's love preeminently, glorifying God in everything and tenderly constraining all those who looked upon him in faith to say in seeing him, "What love there is in God." He demonstrated God's love because he who said to us, "Anyone who has seen me has seen the Father" (John 14:9), is himself filled with such love. And how did he make this love apparent? He made it apparent in everything he did, but above all in suffering for his brothers. He suffered first of all for their temporal deliver-

---

1 Here, Monod is equating light with holiness, and goodness (or benevolence) with love. In the latter case, he would seem to be thinking of the Hebrew concept of *chesed*, God's covenant-keeping love, which the King James Version typically translates as "lovingkindness." In newer translations it is rendered as "love" or "kindness," but the traditional Protestant French translation most often uses the word *bonté*, or "goodness."

ance as he "went about doing good" (Acts 10:38). But these healings were only the types and images of the true deliverance, which is spiritual. Thus he demonstrated God's love above all in suffering for their spiritual deliverance. Likewise, the highest demonstration we can give of the love of God is in suffering for our brothers and particularly for the salvation of their souls. We can all do it, my dear friends.

Not everyone can do it in a special and direct way like the apostle Paul, whose entire life was consecrated to the preaching of the gospel and who said, "I fill up in my flesh what is still lacking in regard to Christ's afflictions, for the sake of his body, which is the church" (Col. 1:24). We do not have to look for an exact interpretation of those words. There is an infinity of kindness, a depth of love in these words of Saint Paul that do not lend themselves to being wrapped up in human definitions. His entire life was filled with the need to imitate his Savior, who left us "an example, that [we] should follow in his steps" (1 Peter 2:21). As his Savior suffered for men in order to save them, Paul feels the need to suffer for his brothers, not to save them (none has declared more clearly than Paul that no man, no created being can do anything to save us), but to work for their salvation, "because if you do, you will save both yourself and your hearers." (1 Tim. 4:16).

SUFFERING TURNED INTO LOVE

But even though we might not have such sufferings as Paul's, directly endured for the service of God and the good of men, there is not one of our sufferings to which we cannot communicate this character by the spirit that we bring to it. Let those of us "who suffer according to the will of God commit their souls to him in doing good, as to a faithful Creator" (1 Peter 4:19 NKJV). Let us apply ourselves to turn our sufferings—those of soul, of spirit, of body; all those that it will please God to send us—to the good of men; to their temporal good and above all to their spiritual good. If we do this we will have attained the purpose for which God sent them to us.

In general, my beloveds, the more we love and the more we walk in this spiritual communion among ourselves and with God, the more we will be like him. Let us go then into the world, each one of us, as a reflection of the divine love. May all our words, our works, our most private thoughts, our most intimate prayers breathe out that love which God has revealed to us in Jesus Christ and may they constrain men to say, "Oh, how God truly is love!"

To read the talks in original
chronological order, go to
the next chapter.

Building Faith

(December 2, 1855)

Remember those earlier days after you had received the light, when you stood your ground in a great contest in the face of suffering. Sometimes you were publicly exposed to insult and persecution; at other times you stood side by side with those who were so treated. You sympathized with those in prison and joyfully accepted the confiscation of your property, because you knew that you yourselves had better and lasting possessions.

So do not throw away your confidence; it will be richly rewarded. You need to persevere so that when you have done the will of God, you will receive what he has promised. For in just a very little while,

"He who is coming will come and will not delay.
But my righteous one will live by faith.

And if he shrinks back,
    I will not be pleased with him."

But we are not of those who shrink back and are destroyed, but of those who believe and are saved.

Hebrews 10:32–39

The faith that is the subject of the few verses that were just read to us and which is also the subject of that admirable eleventh chapter of Hebrews that immediately follows them; the faith of which the sacrament of the Lord's Supper is such a simple and yet profound picture; that faith, my friends, is our only power and our only peace. For faith is nothing less than the power of God placed at man's disposal.

OMNIPOTENT FAITH

In the eleventh chapter of Hebrews, Saint Paul sums up all of the gifts, sanctification as well as prophecy and miracles, in faith alone. He does not say, "How was Moses able to cross the Red Sea? It was by being clothed with supernatural power." Rather he says, "It was because he believed." He does not say, "How was Abraham able to do the great things which he did? It was by a supernatural power." Rather he says, "It was because he believed." Thus we need to appreciate not only that the Holy Spirit explained all the greatest works of the saints by an internal and completely spiritual principle, but even more that he explained them by a principle that is available to all. If, in the end, even in the case of Moses or Abraham, we are told only of faith, then we see that just as they were enabled to accomplish the works

85

that God assigned to them, so each of us can be enabled by that same faith to accomplish the work that God puts before us. The works vary, but the principle by which God accomplishes them in each one of us is the same. It is one. It is divine. It is all-powerful.

Let us not be astounded by this. At first it seems quite astounding that the simple fact of God listening to us and responding can accomplish such wonders, and truly the will of God realized in the humblest Christian is no less a wonder than the crossing of the Red Sea or any other marvel ever accomplished. Yet in reflecting a moment on it, the power of faith is understood in its very nature. Consider the fact that you and I are placed in the midst of this world plunged in sin and are entreated by sight, by feelings, by self-will, by example, and finally by the evidence of our senses. What a marvelous thing that we should be able to set all of that aside and believe one word, one little word that God speaks to us; to believe against hope, against experience, and against sight, irresistible sight. You recall this phrase of Luther, "Ein Wörtlein kann ihn fällen" (One little word can fell him). If that little word of God penetrating into our hearts is faith, it is no wonder that faith is all-powerful, because it is no wonder that God should do all that he desires.

ACQUIRING FAITH

But that faith, which is so great in its effects, so prodigious in its nature that it could only be the creation of God in our souls—after all, a man who believes is more astounding than a new world formed by the hand of God—how can we have it? By asking for it! God gives to him who asks. But here, my dear friends, let us be careful. One could believe that such faith is easy to obtain and that it would be enough, in the moment when you have need of it, to offer a prayer to God in order to obtain it. No, no. The good things of God are not so cheap.

Sometimes, no doubt, it pleases him and demonstrates his nature to create a new man all of a sudden in response to a single prayer, but that is not the usual working of his providence. Faith, though it be granted in response to our prayers, is the result of a long and laborious conquest, and it is well worth it. God wants us to battle to obtain it. Adam said a very true thing in his *Private Thoughts:* "Prayer is the easiest of all works, but the prayer of faith is the hardest."[1] We reach our goal by falling often to our knees, by reiterating our prayers, by showing God that we sense the cost of faith, and by adding practice to prayer. Thus from a first prayer we receive a little bit of faith, which encourages us to make a more fervent prayer that will gain us new faith. We have to do three things to grow in faith: ask for it, put it into practice, and see it in the example of the great saints through a deep study of Scripture. Let us not hope to obtain anything from God if we fail to sense its worth.

INVESTING IN FAITH FOR THE FUTURE

Now here, in a few words, is the main application I want to make from what I just said. It is needful to gather faith for the future; it is needful to work today in order to have the

---

1 Thomas Adam (1701–1784), *Private Thoughts on Religion and Other Subjects Connected with It.* (York, England: T. Wilson and R. Spence, 1803), 204. The exact quote is, "Nothing is more easy than to say the words of prayer; but to pray hungering and thirsting is the hardest of all works."

faith you will need in five, ten, or twenty years; it is needful to amass this spiritual provision day by day. Then, being surrounded by the most abundant gifts of God, you will need only to open your eyes and stretch forth your hands when you reach the time when even the strength to pray will be diminished, when your languishing body and your battered spirit will be less suited to this terrible battle of which faith is the price and the reward.

Ah! Don't wait for those supreme moments to acquire faith, thinking that it can always be found. Rather, let us apply ourselves to anticipate those moments by ever and always accumulating faith and by growing in it every day. My friends, I am in a position where nothing matters to me but faith. It is through faith that we have power and peace and joy, as our brother said in his prayer. Alas, it is easy to speak and to preach at a distance that faith must triumph over all. But when we must battle hand to hand with the enemy, when it is a matter of obtaining everything, when it is a matter of following Jesus Christ first in the morning in the desert, then in the evening in Gethsemane, and then in the afternoon on Golgotha, one senses that it is serious business indeed.

May God be blessed, eternally blessed, you understand me very poorly if you think that because I speak this way, God does not sustain me. He sustains me admirably. But I want you to know in advance that the battle is hard—much more so than I imagined before passing through it—in order that you might do what I did in my small measure and what I now wish I had done to better advantage. I desire that you might grow in faith every day; that you might live for nothing except to increase in faith; that you might be nothing before God but men of faith and prayer, preparing yourselves to do his will tomorrow by doing his will today. Oh, how much my sufferings would be eased, how much they are eased by the thought that they are useful to you, that the words I speak to you in my infirmity have penetrated into your hearts by the Holy Spirit!

Oh, my friends, if we who make up this small handful of men were truly men of faith, there would be many more eleventh chapters of Hebrews to write without ever leaving this upper room!

To read the talks in original
chronological order, go to
chapt. 16 on p. 104.

Seeing the Invisible

(December 30, 1855)

Then the angel showed me the river of the water of life, as clear as crystal, flowing from the throne of God and of the Lamb down the middle of the great street of the city. On each side of the river stood the tree of life, bearing twelve crops of fruit, yielding its fruit every month. And the leaves of the tree are for the healing of the nations. No longer will there by any curse. The throne of God and of the Lamb will be in the city, and his servants will serve him. They will see his face, and his name will be on their foreheads. There will be no more night. They will not need the light of a lamp or the light of the sun, for the Lord God will give them light. And they will reign for ever and ever.

The angel said to me, "These words are trustworthy and true. The Lord, the God of the spirits of the prophets, sent his angel to show his servants the things that must soon take place."

"Behold, I am coming soon! Blessed is he who keeps the words of the prophecy in this book."

I, John, am the one who heard and saw these things. And when I had heard and seen them, I fell down to worship at the feet of the angel who had been showing them to me. But he said to me, "Do not do it! I am a fellow servant with you and with your brothers the prophets and of all who keep the words of this book. Worship God!"

Then he told me, "Do not seal up the words of the prophecy of this book, because the time is near. Let him who does wrong continue to do wrong; let him who is vile continue to be vile; let him who does right continue to do right; and let him who is holy continue to be holy."

"Behold, I am coming soon! My reward is with me, and I will give to everyone according to what he has done. I am the Alpha and the Omega, the First and the Last, the Beginning and the End.

"Blessed are those who wash their robes, that they may have the right to the tree of life and may go through the gates into the city. Outside are the dogs, those who practice magic arts, the sexually immoral, the murderers, the idolaters and everyone who loves and practices falsehood.

"I, Jesus, have sent my angel to give you this testimony for the churches. I am the Root and Offspring of David, and the bright Morning Star."

The Spirit and the bride say, "Come!" And let him who hears say, "Come!" Whoever is thirsty, let him come; and whoever wishes, let him take the free gift of the water of life.

I warn everyone who hears the words of the prophecy of this book: If anyone adds anything to them, God will add to him the plagues described in this book. And if anyone takes words away from this book of prophecy, God will take away from him his share in the tree of life and in the holy city, which are described in this book.

He who testifies to these things says, "Yes, I am coming soon."

Amen. Come Lord Jesus.

The grace of the Lord Jesus be with God's people. Amen.

Revelation 22

The chapter that was just read to us would, by itself, suffice to fill our hearts continually with strength and joy if we could receive it with complete simplicity of faith. If a man pressured by poverty were assured that tomorrow he would make a fortune, or if a man pressured by suffering were assured that tomorrow he would enter into a life of well-being, would they not be sustained to wait a few hours? Would they not by that hope outdistance the few hours that separate them from the moment when they will be happy? And we, my friends, if we had simple, firm faith and a clear perception of that eternal bliss described for us in such beautiful and yet touching terms in the last chapter of Revelation, would we too not say, "Come, Lord Jesus!" and would we not say it with complete peace?

OUR NEED FOR THE INVISIBLE

What do we need more than what God has given us? Nothing but what God can give us again: simple faith in the invisible. We live in time, while it is only a matter of living in eternity. We are constantly drawn toward the visible things, while it is only a matter of entering into communion with the invisible. I say it is *only* a matter of that, but it is still a great thing, an immense change. After all, that which constitutes sin is not only the gross forms of disobedience to divine law that reign in the world. In a more subtle way and a way much closer to its source, that which constitutes sin is unbelief and being drawn away by the visible things. The only reason that we have so much difficulty in feeding on the invisible things is that we are naturally far from God, for God is invisible and the center and soul of the invisible realm.

It is the nature of the Word of God that it lives and moves in the midst of the invisible. That alone, for a thinking man, would suffice to prove its inspiration. It is not given to man, slave as he is through his fallen nature to visible things, to lift himself above them. He cannot get out of himself in order to lift himself up to the invisible realm and to speak from its midst as the Word of God does. It is Jesus Christ, the Son of man, who, being in heaven, speaks from heaven; and not only he but also the instruments charged with transmitting the Word of God to us. That Word, being filled with Jesus Christ, speaks from heaven though remaining on earth. It does so through that marvel of the grace of God that we call inspiration and that gives it its authority. Pure book. Holy book. Book of God. Book that itself is lifted above us and the world, that speaks to us of another world from the heart of another world.

How will we be put in touch with the invisible? On this particular point we all sense our need and our weakness. But do we sense how great would be our power, our happiness, our peace, and our joy if we were able, like the Word of God and like Jesus Christ, to live and move in the midst of the invisible things? Do we sense what it would be like if we were able, through the power of faith, to be transported ahead of time into God and into the things of God so as to see things as God sees them, to measure them with his measure, to appreciate them with his appreciation, and to judge them as he judges them? "If we judged ourselves, we would not come under judgment" (1 Cor. 11:31) was just quoted to us as coming from God.

LIVE WITH THE SCRIPTURES

From what we have just seen, the first way to put ourselves in touch with the invisible realm is to live with the Holy Scriptures, which are the Word and the testimony of God. By *live* with them, I do not mean simply to read them every day and to receive their testimony. I mean to nourish ourselves with them; to search there for the bread of life that is come down from heaven; to search there for the Lord Jesus Christ, that life-giving bread, who gives life to the world and whose flesh was broken for you, for me, for us all. I mean, too, that we should receive him by faith, in particular in the sacrament of the Lord's Supper, which puts the object of our faith so vividly before our eyes.

We must feed on God's Word, my dear friends. We must live with it constantly, day and night. May it be for us what it was (to cite only one example) for the author of Psalm 119—that psalm with 176 verses of which not more than two or three fail to mention the Word of God with one of those countless names the psalmist gives it. Ah, let us live with the Word of God! Let us be constantly surrounded by the atmosphere of the Scriptures, for this is the atmosphere of heaven and of God himself!

PRAY WITHOUT CEASING

To put ourselves in contact with the invisible, let us also pray without ceasing. Yes, pray. But how to pray? Oh, my God, to pray as if seeing you, as if talking to you, listening to you, answering you; as if sensing your presence and savoring your Word. Oh, who will teach us to pray if it is not you, God of prayer?

My God, forgive the way in which your church, which alone in the world knows enough to pray, does pray. Forgive the way in which we ourselves pray; the half-heartedness, the uncertainty, the unbelief we exhibit even on the least un-faithful, the least unbelieving days of our Christian life and ministry! My God, forgive the sin of our holy offerings!

Ah, if only we could, right now through prayer, cross the distance that separates us from you; if we could pray as Jesus Christ prayed, as Moses prayed, or Samuel, or David, or Saint Paul, or Saint John! If only we could pray that which is called praying—that which is called praying!—according to that expression that Saint James uses in speaking of Elijah: "he prayed in prayer" (James 5:17 KJV, marginal reading).

Alas, most of the time we pray without praying. We have no idea of the weakness and unbelief that are mingled with our prayers for want of living with the invisible. We have no idea of the blessings and favors of which we deprive our-selves. Oh, my friends, let us constantly repeat this prayer, "Lord, teach us to pray!" When we know how to pray, we will know all, and, what is of even greater worth, we will have all. We will know Jesus, and we will do better than simply know him; we will possess him. Besides, one knows him only in possessing him. It is in possessing him that one knows him, and in knowing him that one loves him and that one triumphs with him by faith over the visible world and crushes Satan under foot. May the God of peace crush Satan beneath our feet!

THE NEED IS NOW

My friends, the invisible things, the things of the last chapter of Revelation! . . . Soon we are going to appear before God. This is not only true of those who wait from day to day to be called—those who are specifically warned by the Lord to keep themselves ready and who rejoice, who long ardently for the moment when Jesus will say to them, "Come!" It is equally true for all, since not one of us is assured that he will live until evening. It is now, it is while you have free use of all your faculties that you must put yourselves in touch with the invisible realm through the Word of God and through prayer.

These are very old things I am telling you, but, alas, very new through our unbelief and our indifference! . . . Seek the invisible things. Seek God seated in the midst of this invisible world. Seek him through Jesus Christ, who has opened the way for us through the veil, that is, through his broken body. His love and his suffering are the measure of the joy that he has prepared for us! "Though it linger, wait for it; it will certainly come and will not delay" (Hab. 2:3).

To read the talks in original
chronological order, go to
chapt. 18 on p. 118.

part 4
WHEN HARD TIMES COME

When peace, like a river, attendeth my way,
When sorrows like sea billows roll;
Whatever my lot, thou hast taught me to say,
It is well, it is well with my soul.

Though Satan should buffet, though trials should
    come,
Let this blest assurance control:
That Christ hath regarded my helpless estate
And hath shed his own blood for my soul.

                                    Horatio Gates Spafford
                                           1828–1888

uffering as he was from terminal cancer, it is
not surprising that a number of Adolphe
Monod's teachings should deal directly with the
question of suffering. How could they not? Yet his fo-
cus is positive and upward; his mood is one of peace and
even joy.

These talks were originally interspersed among those of
the previous section but have been grouped together for the
benefit of those readers who may be facing hard times.

BENEFITS HIDDEN IN PAIN

(November 4, 1855)

Praise be to the God and Father of our Lord Jesus Christ, the Father of compassion and the God of all comfort, who comforts us in all our troubles, so that we can comfort those in any trouble with the comfort we ourselves have received from God. For just as the sufferings of Christ flow over into our lives, so also through Christ our comfort overflows. If we are distressed, it is for your comfort and salvation; if we are comforted, it is for your comfort, which produces in you patient endurance of the same sufferings we suffer. And our hope for you is firm, because we know that just as you share in our sufferings, so also you share in our comfort.

2 Corinthians 1:3–7

What a mercy of God that he should give us in communion a picture that is so simple and at the same time so pro-

found of the invisible grace of the Lord! If we gather together all the lessons that Scripture gives us on the subject,
we see that the whole foundation of the gospel is on that
table, for we find two things there. First we find Jesus Christ
dying for us. That death, that blood, that atoning sacrifice is
the unique hope of our salvation, accomplishing absolutely
everything for the elect of God. Then, what is more, we find
there this dead Jesus penetrating inside of us and nourishing
us; communicating life to us by his flesh and blood. Thus he
makes us to be participants in his nature just as he is a par-
ticipant in the Father's nature. Now our aim is to die to ourselves and to live to Christ by the Holy Spirit, seeing that
Jesus Christ died for us on the cross. This is the whole of the
gospel, the whole of faith, the whole Christian life.

I would like to add a few words here that I give not in a
personal sense but in the sense in which Saint Paul said,
"Let no one become slack because of the sufferings I endure" (see Eph. 3:13). To be sure, I have no intention of
comparing those afflictions, which were so great and so directly endured for the service of God, with the sufferings
God has had the grace to visit on me. But I do desire, by the
spirit in which I accept them, to turn them into an affliction
endured for the sake of the gospel and also, in some small
measure, for you.

BENEFITS TO THOSE IN PAIN

I don't want anyone to become disheartened. Perhaps
some of my good friends are troubled by the thought of what
I am suffering. Well, don't be. Give me this token of your
brotherly love, that rather than being troubled, you would
experience a healthy excitement and expectancy. It is not

that I don't suffer or that I don't suffer in suffering. I am not a stoic. By the grace of God I am a Christian, and I am not ashamed to say that there are moments when I pray far less than I cry out in tears. I remember that my Savior also uttered loud cries with tears. But while these things are painful to the flesh, they are accompanied by such great blessings that a sense of gratitude must rule in my heart and in yours.

What a gift it is to me, dear friends, that God, in desiring to use one of us to remind the others of the lessons of life and of the concepts of death, sin, grace, and sanctification, should have condescended to choose me! What a privilege that in taking me he should have spared my brothers, and what a privilege that he should choose me to give you these lessons on eternal life! Think about how what is happening to me is suited to make me appreciate a Christian removal at whatever moment it might come to me.[1] Let us all seek only to glorify God. If it please him to heal me, I ask only that it might be for his glory. If he wants to take me, I will be happy to be gathered into his bosom. I cannot know which would be better either for me or for the church. I abandon myself completely to him. But what a gift for me to have been selected to be thus matured through suffering! You have good reason to rejoice for me.

BENEFITS FOR THOSE AROUND THEM

As for yourselves, is it not true that my affliction has led you to think about death, about eternity, about the truths of

---

1 The word translated "removal" has the sense of moving out of a dwelling place—normally a house or an apartment but in this case the physical body, the "earthly house of this tabernacle" (2 Cor. 5:1 KJV).

the gospel? Have you not been pushed to prayer by the brotherly love that unites us? I sense that I have been carried by the prayers of God's people, and because of this I am filled with joy and pierced with gratitude. Well, then, is there not great benefit for you in that? Do you not sense that everything that happens to me can cause a spirit of peace and serenity to flow over my immediate society and most especially over my family? Do you not sense that our house has become, to a greater degree than ever before, a house of prayer, a house where the name of God is being constantly invoked, even as others are constantly invoking his name on its behalf? Thus there are many blessings to appropriate.

Please understand how much sweetness I find in the thought that I am afflicted for your good, because nothing could better make my sufferings approach those of my Savior. Thus I say in the spirit of this same Saint Paul whom I have already quoted, "Now I rejoice in what was suffered for you, and I fill up in my flesh what is still lacking in regard to Christ's afflictions, for the sake of his body, which is the church" (Col. 1:24).

Help in the Battle Against Sin

Oh, marvel of the grace of God! Power of the gospel! Bitterness of sin! Unchangeable firmness of grace! Let us battle against sin, my friends; that is the only evil, that is the only evil. Now that I find myself face to face with sin, now that I find myself called to review before God all the sins of my life and to ask his forgiveness of them, I sense how awful this battle is, how deeply rooted sin is, and how absurd it would be for us to complain of the troubles God sends us. Even these troubles do not suffice to uproot that miserable pride, that terrible self-centeredness, and, above all, that detestable unbelief. May the peace of God be with us.

Put aside all personal feelings. Do not see the father or the friend in me, or at least see them only to a limited degree. Rather see in me, before all else, the minister of Jesus Christ and ask God to keep me faithful in this ministry right up to my last breath. Do not see the man in me, but see the work that God desires to accomplish in me and in you. Let us take courage. Let us ask God to fill us with his Spirit, to enable us to overcome the flesh by the spirit while waiting for him to gather us up from the presence of evil. Let us pray that, through Jesus Christ, God might allow us to taste, in a spiritual body and a sanctified soul, the joy, the delights, and the glory that the shed blood of Jesus Christ alone has merited for us!

To read the talks in original
chronological order, go to
chapt. 10 on p. 70.

16

The View from Beneath the Cross

(December 9, 1855)

And we know that in all things God works for the good of those who love him, who have been called according to his purpose. For those God foreknew he also predestined to be conformed to the likeness of his Son, that he might be the firstborn among many brothers. And those he predestined, he also called; those he called, he also justified; those he justified he also glorified. What, then, shall we say in response to this? If God is for us, who can be against us?

Romans 8:28–31

In the presence of Jesus Christ, who nourishes us with his flesh and his blood and who nourishes us continually by faith, I have it on my heart to speak a few words to those who suffer. I am quite sure that, no matter how small my audience may be, my remarks will fall on soil prepared to receive them. We all suffer. Furthermore, those who suffer the most are not always those who seem to suffer the most. There are pains and sorrows[1] known unto God and unknown to men. In any case all who feel, all who think, all who believe, have a deep acquaintance with the nature of suffering.

There is something in suffering that is quite contrary to our nature and to which it is very difficult for us to adjust, for it seems to us that we should always be happy. This feeling is entirely legitimate and honors the goodness of our Creator. It is perfectly true that we should be completely exempt from pain and ever filled with joy, but sin has disturbed all that, so that now what was contrary to nature has become natural. It has now entered into God's plan as well as into our everyday experience and our eternal interest that we should suffer in a variety of ways. You know how Job's experience brings together and classifies the major troubles of life: loss of goods, loss of those who are dear to us, and loss of health, which is reserved for last; or rather that order comes from Satan, who is an expert in temptations. If, at this moment, the hearts of all of us here were opened, what pains and sorrows would we not have to tell to God!

THE SOURCE OF CONSOLATION

Very well, my dear friends, I would have absolutely nothing with which to console you if I did not take it from God's

---

1 The French word here rendered as "pains and sorrows" is *douleurs*, which can be translated either as "pains" in the sense of physical pains or as "sorrows," which can be thought of as emotional or spiritual pains. Both are probably in view in this text. Elsewhere in this chapter *douleur* is also translated "suffering."

Word. There is no consolation in nature. It explains nothing; it understands nothing; it hopes nothing; it expects nothing, for even its hope and expectation are empty.

But I am full of things to say to you while meditating on the cross of Jesus Christ around which we are gathered to celebrate the memory of his sacrifice. We are cleansed from our sins by his blood—you know it well—cleansed from our sins by his blood, redeemed by his bitter sacrifice, our sins having been atoned for by his cross. In the simplest, commonest, yet most profound sense, Jesus Christ is the propitiatory sacrifice who reconciles us to God by his death. That is the foundation of the gospel; that is its heart, and apart from it there is only an eroded and impotent gospel. But beneath the cross, the whole appearance of pain changes, and it changes in proportion to our faith.

MADE LIKE CHRIST

Jesus Christ, the Son of God, appeared in the world. But how did he appear? As a man of joy? No, as a man of sorrows. It is a marvel, something astonishing and contrary to the natural order: the Son of God appearing on earth and appearing there not only as suffering, but as suffering things that none can imagine by way of suffering. The cross of Jesus Christ is the center of all pain and sorrow. It absorbs them all; there is not one that does not naturally flow forth from it; there is none that the cross of Jesus Christ does not explain to us.

My dear friends, we need to recall that Jesus Christ has suffered for us; we need to consider that everything we suffer is a similarity to our Savior and that because of the infinite nature of his suffering we resemble him all the more as our sufferings increase. Isn't it true that when we do that, the nature of pain is changed? Is it not a luminous yet sweet thought that Jesus Christ bore pain before us and that he could not be spared from it?

Who is the one, beaten down though he may be, who would not be sustained by the thought: "It is like my Savior; it is a similarity to him. Now I know that I belong to him and that he calls me. I know that I am beginning to enter into God's plan and to understand his ways. I unite my cross to his cross and my suffering to his suffering." This is why Saint Paul says, "For those God foreknew he also predestined to be conformed to the likeness of his Son, that he might be the firstborn among many brothers. And those he predestined, he also called; those he called, he also justified; those he justified, he also glorified" (Rom. 8:29–30). He desired that we might be "conformed to the likeness of his Son," and the context shows us that we are here dealing essentially with a conformity of suffering. This is a first thought that is powerful enough to sustain us: pain is an essential part of the life of Jesus Christ, and it is thus a resemblance to him.

FREED FROM SIN'S POWER

Here is another. Why did Jesus Christ suffer? To atone for sin. Thus suffering appears before us as a righteous consequence of sin. We cannot bear the sufferings that Jesus Christ bore, but we will be happy to bear our part in a spirit of justice and punishment. "Why should any living man complain when punished for his sins?" (Lam. 3:39). Consider this passage from Saint Peter: "Therefore, since Christ suffered in his body, arm yourselves also with the same attitude, because he who has suffered in his body is done with

107

sin" (1 Peter 4:1). This shows us that in order for us to be able to break away from sin, we must suffer.

For our sake and in our person, sin and suffering must be set face to face; pain must be used to destroy the sin in us, not as an atonement for sin—that is found only in Jesus Christ—but so that we may learn to unite pain with sin and joy with sanctification and deliverance. Very well, then, this thought that pain is a fruit of sin is able to sustain us because it makes us consider pain as a simple and natural path from which we could not and should not be spared.

ABLE TO DEMONSTRATE GOD'S LOVE

Finally, why did Jesus Christ suffer as an atonement for sin? In order to save us and to make us participants in eternal glory through love. That is the thought that dominates in the Savior's sufferings. Well, then, our suffering must also be the suffering of love and not of egoism; it must not draw our attention to ourselves but draw it first of all to God, that he might be glorified, and then to our neighbor, that he might be benefited. Love's treasures and love's power are present in Christian suffering through the example that a believer can give, through the patience with which God enables him to bear it. What a sweet, heavenly thought that in suffering we can be useful and, above all, useful to our brothers! What could better bring our sufferings together with those of Christ?

That is the thought that Saint Paul expresses when he says in a passage I am fond of citing, "I fill up in my flesh what is still lacking in regard to Christ's afflictions, for the sake of his body, which is the church" (Col. 1:24). I will not go into the explanation of this verse, which presents some difficulties. Most assuredly Saint Paul was never dreaming of suffering for the atonement of sin, but he unites his sufferings with those of the Savior, and because Christ had suffered to save us, so Paul suffers for the good of humanity. Thus he writes to Timothy, "In doing this you will save both yourself and those who hear you" (1 Tim. 4:16 NKJV).

Freedom from Self, Joy in Christ

That is what sustains the Christian in suffering. Jesus Christ suffered: thus the more I suffer, the more I am like him, so suffering is a privilege. Jesus Christ suffered for sin: thus pain is a necessary and healthy fruit of sin. Finally, Jesus Christ suffered to save: thus I too must suffer to do good to men and to lead captive souls to the obedience of the cross.

May all those who suffer strive to get out of themselves, to reject a self-centered suffering, without faith, without love, and also without consolation. May they strive to enter fully into the love of Christ so that their pain, too, might be like a cross planted on the earth, whose shadow would shelter those around them, not to give them eternal life but to show them the pathway that leads there, to the glory of God. To him be the glory for ever and ever!

Let us rejoice in him, and let us affirm that through the power of faith and love there is no suffering that cannot be peacefully and happily endured and that cannot be related to the glory of God and the good of men. This will so work to our eternal consolation that in heaven we will consider it a great privilege to have suffered much beneath the cross of Jesus! Amen.

To read the talks in original
chronological order, go to
chapt. 2 on p. 11.

When God Seems Absent

(December 23, 1855)

O LORD, the God who saves me,
    day and night I cry out before you.
May my prayer come before you;
    turn your ear to my cry.

For my soul is full of trouble
    and my life draws near the grave.
I am counted among those who go down to the pit;
    I am like a man without strength.
I am set apart with the dead,
    like the slain who lie in the grave,
whom you remember no more,
    who are cut off from your care.

You have put me in the lowest pit,
    in the darkest depths.

Your wrath lies heavily upon me;
  you have overwhelmed me with all your waves.
You have taken me from my closest friends
  and have made me repulsive to them.
I am confined and cannot escape;
  my eyes are dim with grief.

I call to you, O LORD, every day;
  I spread out my hands to you.
Do you show your wonders to the dead?
  Do those who are dead rise up and praise you?
Is your love declared in the grave,
  your faithfulness in Destruction?
Are your wonders known in the place of darkness,
  or your righteous deeds in the land of oblivion?

But I cry to you for help, O LORD;
  in the morning my prayer comes before you.
Why, O LORD, do you reject me
  and hide your face from me?

From my youth I have been afflicted and close to
      death;
  I have suffered your terrors and am in despair.
Your wrath has swept over me;
  your terrors have destroyed me.
All day long they surround me like a flood;
  they have completely engulfed me.
You have taken my companions and loved ones
      from me;
  the darkness is my closest friend.

                                        Psalm 88

My good friends, you give me such a touching mark of your affection and your brotherly concern by coming to share the Lord's Supper with me as from week to week it nourishes and strengthens me in spirit and body.

WHEN ALL SEEMS DARK

There is in Psalm 88, which was read at the opening of the service, a feature that is unique among all of the psalms: it is the only one that is completely in pain and that does not end with a word or hint of consolation. It is completely black, completely somber, and one must look very closely at it to discover even a seed of hope contained in a name given to God in one of the first verses: "the God who saves us." Why this astounding mystery? I find two explanations.

First, God wanted to make us see that while in the usual working of his mercy, we never cry out to him without being delivered, and while it often requires no more than the space of a few verses in the psalms to cross the gap that separates the most frightful anguish from the most abundant comfort (as in Ps. 13), yet it can occasionally enter into the Lord's purposes to let us cry out for a certain period of time without an answer, without consolation, and without so much as a poor, isolated little ray of light coming to brighten our distress. Those are the times when we must be nourished by faith alone. Along with Jeremiah, with David, and with all of the saints who have been similarly tested, we must wait for God. We must ask him why he hides himself, and in spite of the cloud that conceals him from us, we must never doubt him. In 150 psalms, there is *one* that gives us this lesson, as if it cost much for the Lord's love to provide us that warning.

But there is a second explanation of this psalm that is nonetheless related to the first. You know that the psalms are full of Messiah. It is Christ who speaks, who paints his sorrows, and we find in Psalm 88 the same Savior who said in Psalm 22, "Eloi, Eloi, lama sabachthani," "My God, my God, why have you forsaken me?" (Ps. 22:1) followed immediately by the statements: "Yet you are enthroned as the Holy One" (Ps. 22:3); "You listen to the afflicted one who cries out to you" (see Ps. 22:24). Thus this psalm makes us see that there is in the Savior an enormous distress that exceeds all that men, even his most tested servants, can even imagine, let alone experience. And why? Because God is love. Strange answer, but true.

CHRIST'S DARKNESS, OUR LIGHT

God is love. But for us, my dear friends, though we may be filled with the gifts of God, temporal and spiritual and every other kind, though we may be filled with his Word, with his promises, and with all the rest, there is something lacking in God's love (if one may speak this way) for it to be able to find its way into our hearts. That something is pain.

We know that God does not suffer, that he is incapable of suffering, that he is lifted up above pain just as he is above temptation and all the anguishes of earth. Yet in order for us to understand God's love in all of its fullness and reality, it was necessary for God to present himself to us in such a way as to prove his love to us through pain. Mankind could never have been persuaded—or rather won—in any other way. Therefore Jesus Christ, the Son of God and God himself, became the Son of man that he might suffer and thus show us God's love through acts capable of breaking the hardest hearts, inattentive though they might be. Jesus came to earth to suffer. How well he fulfilled that task!

HIS EARTHLY LIFE

He began by putting on a flesh similar to our sinful flesh. Which of us can conceive of the level of abasement, of renunciation, and of sacrifice required for the Lord of glory, the Prince of life to descend into the misery of our poor nature and to accept all of its humiliations, right up to those of the tomb? "Who, being in very nature God, did not consider equality with God something to be grasped, but made himself nothing, taking the very nature of a servant, being made in human likeness. And being found in appearance as a man, he humbled himself and became obedient to death—even death on a cross!" (Phil. 2:6–8).

Note that what distinguishes the pain and sacrifice of Jesus Christ from ours is that he voluntarily chose and summoned them. Nothing required it of him. He chose them and summoned them, one after the other, in order to accomplish the Father's will, and to accomplish it freely. Why? For us, because he could not stand the thought of the eternal misery to which sin had delivered us up. What love, my God, what love!

HIS FINAL STRUGGLE

I pass rapidly over his entire career of pain and humiliation, and I come to his Gethsemane. You enter an olive garden in the middle of the night, and you see a man stretched out with his face to the ground. He weeps. He cries out. Per-

haps you take him for a madman. That is your Savior! Judge
for yourselves the immensity of this suffering from his position, from his prayer, from the tender reproaches addressed
to his disciples. We can no more experience or conceive of
such suffering than we can experience or conceive of God
and the infinite, because there is not only the physical, external suffering, but also a spiritual suffering of which we
can have no conception.

Not only saints, but even men who do not know the
Lord have patiently suffered the most atrocious pains, but in
Jesus, with his infinite pains, there was a secret, inner pain
that we are unable to penetrate. It is the pain of carrying
alone the weight of our sins before the holy God—he the innocent for us the guilty. It is the pain of finding himself as if
separated by them for a moment (though I scarcely dare to
touch on this mystery), separated for a moment from the
love of the Father (if one can speak in these terms) though
remaining one with him, and forced to cry out, "My God,
my God, why have you forsaken me?" Why does he suffer
thus? For you, sinner, for you. And he loved you so much
that if there were none but you to save on earth, he would
have entered his Gethsemane for you. What love, my God,
what love!

Finally, look at him on the cross. I will not dwell at
length on this. Even if I had the strength, how can you describe such a mystery? I place myself with you at the foot of
the cross, and I contemplate my Savior's suffering. Here I
would have you notice something. In the moment when he
is delivered up to this frightful anguish, to this agony that no
man has been able to understand or conceive or even
glimpse, Jesus conquers that pain in order to glorify God
and to save men right up to the end. It is from the heart of

this agony that one hears such words as these come forth: "Father, forgive them, for they do not know what they are doing" (Luke 23:34), and again: "Dear woman, here is your son. . . . Disciple, here is your mother" (John 19:26–27). What love, my God, what love!

FINDING PEACE IN THE DEPTHS OF GOD'S LOVE

Last Sunday, we contemplated at the foot of the cross something of the horror, the enormity, and the terrors of sin.[1] Today, it is sweet to consider in the sufferings of our Savior the vision they give us of the incomprehensible grandeur and depth of God's mercy. Oh, my friends, let us always have that love before our eyes and everything will be explained to us, even the cruelest sufferings, which are nothing but the sequels in our lives of that which he suffered. At the same time, everything will be sweet and easy for us. Faith makes everything possible; love makes everything easy. "His commands are not burdensome" (1 John 5:3).

Full of this picture of the Savior's love and of God's love revealed in the Savior, reading God's love for us in the Father's heart, we will abandon ourselves to the Lord to do and to suffer all that he will judge good to send us. Ask God for the gift of filling you with this thought: "God is love." In order to fill ourselves with it, let us keep ourselves at the foot of our Savior's cross. Let us never lose it from sight until, after having made us to suffer a little (seeing that this is needful), he will take us by the hand, lead us across that interval between Friday and Sunday morning, raise us up with him,

1 See chapter 2 on page 11.

and establish us with him in the realm of glory where he awaits us. There we will bless him all the more for having suffered more and, above all, for having suffered for his name's sake! Amen.

To read the talks in original
chronological order, go to
chapt. 14 on p. 90.

Man of Sorrow, Men of Sorrow

(January 6, 1856)

> Dear friends, do not be surprised at the painful trial
> you are suffering, as though something strange were
> happening to you. But rejoice that you participate in
> the sufferings of Christ, so that you may be overjoyed
> when his glory is revealed.
>
> 1 Peter 4:12–13

The Christian in affliction is directly called of God to
contemplate the place that suffering occupies in the plan of
divine redemption, in the development of the reign of God
on earth, and in the revelation of the Holy Scriptures. It is
thus that he understands that simple yet profound statement, "Dear friends, do not be surprised at the painful trial
you are suffering, as though something strange were happening to you." What would be strange would be if we could

be matured for eternal life, and more particularly, if a servant of God could see himself blessed in his work, I would say not only without afflictions but also without a large measure of afflictions. "We must go through many hardships to enter the kingdom of God" (Acts 14:22).

This doctrine is first of all clearly revealed to us even in the one whose sacrifice we are celebrating right now. We owe our possession of eternal life solely to these sufferings and this sacrifice. The Savior was "a man of sorrows, and acquainted with grief" (Isa. 53:3 KJV). Not just a man of sorrows, but *the man* of sorrows, in whom all sorrows were united and who suffered that which no man could ever either suffer or imagine.[1]

But as the Master, so too the disciples. The disciples of our Lord Jesus Christ (I speak especially of those inspired instruments in whom the Lord has most particularly been manifested and almost even reproduced) have been, I would say, a series of men of sorrows, from Abel right up to Saint Paul and Saint John. This is not sufficiently striking at a superficial study of Scripture, but as one goes deeper in his study of the Word of God, one is more and more struck by it. The apostles, the prophets are presented to us throughout Scripture as men of sorrows, and of greater sorrows than we see or know, for Scripture leaves more to be inferred than what it shows us. To show us what these men of God suffered, it would need to recount the story of their lives in detail.

---

1 The word translated as "sorrows" is again the French word *douleurs*, which can signify "pains" or "sorrows" or both together, which would constitute "suffering." All three words are used in this chapter to translate *douleurs*.

THE APOSTLES

Consider the apostles. There is only one among them whose life is given to us with some measure of detail, but this is a man whose ministry was defined by God in terms of his sorrows. God even said in calling him, "I will show him how much he must suffer for my name" (Acts 9:16). If we follow Saint Paul through the course of his life, we find that it was from beginning to end nothing but a life of external and internal pain. Hear what he himself says in the last verses of 2 Corinthians 11:

> Are they servants of Christ? (I am out of my mind to talk like this.) I am more. I have worked much harder, been in prison more frequently, been flogged more severely, and been exposed to death again and again. Five times I received from the Jews the forty lashes minus one. Three times I was beaten with rods, once I was stoned, three times I was shipwrecked, I spent a night and a day in the open sea, I have been constantly on the move. I have been in danger from rivers, in danger from bandits, in danger from my own countrymen, in danger from Gentiles; in danger in the city, in danger in the country, in danger at sea; and in danger from false brothers. I have labored and toiled and have often gone without sleep; I have known hunger and thirst and have often gone without food; I have been cold and naked. Besides everything else, I face daily the pressure of my concern for all the churches. Who is weak, and I do not feel weak? Who is led into sin, and I do not inwardly burn? (vv. 23–29)

Weigh each detail separately. What a picture! What an outward and inward life! See the measure of his love in the measure of his suffering.

THE PROPHETS

Consider the prophets. "Brothers, as an example of patience in the face of suffering, take the prophets who spoke in the name of the Lord," said Saint James (James 5:10). If we study the lives of the prophets with some degree of attention, and particularly those whose stories we know a bit less imperfectly, we will find that statement to be precisely true. It is true, for example, of Jeremiah, a prophet a few of whose actions are known to us. But of all the prophets, the one who is best known to us is David. His is the story that is given to us in greatest detail.

Have you ever reflected on the sorrows that filled David's life? If you take his life as it is presented to us in 1 and 2 Samuel and also in Kings and Chronicles, you will know nothing of them. You see in David a man who was pursued in his early life by Saul and who had many enemies but who finally triumphed over Saul and inherited great glory. Next you see this man deeply afflicted and beaten down in the heart of his family as a just consequence of his sins, but you also see him abundantly consoled and sustained by God. Even in the midst of his most awesome punishments, God remembers once again his promises to David and his mercy toward him. It is a life in which we find many trials and agitations, but in the end it does not give us the sense of David's sorrows.

You have to read the psalms in order to know David's sorrows. The psalms reveal David's inner man, and in

David's inner man they in some measure show us the inner man of all the prophets of God. We find that the psalms are filled with expressions of unheard of sorrow. There David speaks continually of his troubles, his sicknesses, and his countless enemies. In reading them one can scarcely understand what he means by these enemies of whom he is always speaking, but they at least reveal to us an inner affliction that we would never have suspected with only the story of David available. That is one of the great uses of the psalms.

Read Psalm 38 and weigh each bit of it:

Oh LORD, do not rebuke me in your anger
    or discipline me in your wrath.
For your arrows have pierced me,
    and your hand has come down upon me.
Because of your wrath there is no health in my
        body;
    my bones have no soundness because of my sin.
My guilt has overwhelmed me
    like a burden too heavy to bear.

My wounds fester and are loathsome
    because of my sinful folly.
I am bowed down and brought very low;
    all day long I go about mourning.
My back is filled with searing pain;
    there is no health in my body.
I am feeble and utterly crushed;
    I groan in anguish of heart.

All my longings lie open before you, O Lord;
    my sighing is not hidden from you.

My heart pounds, my strength fails me;
    even the light has gone from my eyes.
My friends and companions avoid me because of
      my wounds;
    my neighbors stay far away.
Those who seek my life set their traps,
    those who would harm me talk of my ruin;
    all day long they plot deception.

I am like a deaf man, who cannot hear,
    like a mute, who cannot open his mouth;
I have become like a man who does not hear,
    whose mouth can offer no reply.
I wait for you, O LORD;
    you will answer, O Lord my God.
For I said, "Do not let them gloat
    or exalt themselves over me when my foot
      slips."

For I am about to fall,
    and my pain is ever with me.
I confess my iniquity;
    I am troubled by my sin.
Many are those who are my vigorous enemies;
    those who hate me without reason are numerous.
Those who repay my good with evil
    slander me when I pursue what is good.

O LORD, do not forsake me;
    be not far from me, O my God.
Come quickly to help me,
    O Lord my Savior.

The countless enemies who come against him, the sense of his sins that overwhelms him, that complexity of ills (he is struck in the eyes, from which he loses light; his loins are inflamed; his body is bent over so that he can scarcely walk; and his running sores give off an awful odor)—such is David in this psalm. But if you read Psalm 6, if you read Psalm 69, if you read a number of psalms, you will find him in similar afflictions. There, truly, is a man overcome with sorrows.

It is not necessarily true that because David was a type for Jesus Christ his sorrows apply only to the Messiah. No doubt David's sorrows were a type for those of Jesus Christ, but they could only have been a type for the Messiah's sorrows because they were sorrows. It is precisely because David was a man of sorrows that he was a type for *the* man of sorrows.

Conquerors, All

But, my dear friends, shall we leave things there? Having recognized that the apostles and prophets were men of sorrows, shall we leave things with that sad thought of pain? Not at all! They were not only men of sorrows, but they were men who conquered pain and made their suffering work to the glory of God.

Jesus Christ, at the head of those who belong to him, triumphs over suffering and pursues his mission of love even through the cruelest anguish. In Gethsemane, we hear him exhorting his disciples and preserving all his freedom of spirit as he fulfills his message of love near them. It is the same on the cross where he never misses a chance to give the lessons of eternal life to his disciples, to the people, to John, to Mary, to all. And he continues to do so right up to the end of his awful agony. This is the man of sorrows triumphing over pain in order to accomplish his mission in and through his suffering.

It is the same with his disciples. It is the same with his apostles. What use does Saint Paul make of his sorrows? He turns each one to the glory of God. He is in no sense overcome by his sufferings, as we so easily are. He triumphs over them through the goodness of Christ and makes them all work for the advancement of God's rule with a marvelous fidelity.

And David, with whom I have been particularly concerned; have you noticed how he triumphs over his sorrows in order to do his work? The main object of David's mission from God, for all generations in the church, is the composition of the psalms. Well, he composes the psalms, or a large number of them, in the midst of the cruelest sorrows.

Imagine that you, being overcome by physical, moral, and spiritual suffering, are called upon to write a psalm and that from the heart of all this suffering, at the very moment when it is such as he describes it in Psalm 38, what comes forth are hymns to the glory of God and for the instruction of the church. What a victory for David over himself, and what a humiliation for us who, in our weakness, are most often obliged to wait until our sufferings have passed before we can gather in their fruit and let it be gathered for others! Yet David writes his psalms in his pains. He writes his Psalm 38 while he is suffering those persecutions, those inner torments, that bitterness of sin.

I know that one could argue that David wrote Psalm 38 cold, transporting himself back into sorrows that he was no longer experiencing just as a poet transports himself into sorrows he has never known. But no! That supposition is as repugnant to you as it is to me. It is in the furnace, it is from the heart of the furnace that he wrote these lines destined to serve for the encouragement of the church in all ages. Oh, power of the love of Christ! Oh, renouncing of self-will! Oh, grace of the true servant of God! Oh, virtue of the apostle and virtue of the prophet; virtue of Christ in them and of the Holy Spirit! For never would man be capable of such strength of will and of such triumph over the flesh!

Two Questions

My dear friends, I leave to each of you the application, and it comes in the form of two questions. Are we men of sorrows, and in what measure do we share the afflictions of Christ? And when we share Christ's afflictions, do we know how to triumph over them so that, by the power of love, we might turn our afflictions to the glory of God as well as to the good of our neighbor and our brothers even as they work that much more to sanctify us, nourish us, and amass for us the treasure of an excellent glory?

To read the talks in original
chronological order, go to
the next chapter.

AVOIDING REGRETS

Dear Lord and Father of mankind,
Forgive our foolish ways!
Reclothe us in our rightful mind;
In purer lives thy service find,
In deeper reverence, praise.

Drop thy still dews of quietness,
Till all our strivings cease;
Take from our souls the strain and stress,
And let our ordered lives confess
The beauty of thy peace.

John Greenleaf Whittier
1807–1892

We are all imperfect creatures living imperfect lives, and Adolphe Monod was no different. He gave this next series of talks on the things he wished he had done differently or better in his life. Again, however, the emphasis is positive, not negative. He does not dwell on past shortcomings but only desires that he, his friends, and his family might learn from them in order to live lives more pleasing to God.

A Holy, Active, Peaceful Life

(January 13, 1856)

For you are great and do marvelous deeds;
   you alone are God.

Teach me your way, O LORD,
   and I will walk in your truth;
give me an undivided heart,
   that I may fear your name.
I will praise you, O Lord my God, with all my heart;
   I will glorify your name forever.
For great is your love toward me;
   you have delivered me from the depths of the
      grave.

Psalm 86:10–13

My dearly beloved in the dearly beloved of the Father, I
thank God, who again allows me to speak to you in his name

for your encouragement and for my own consolation. But I need to have you exhibit toward me the patience of God, with whom we are acceptable "according to what one has, not according to what he does not have" (2 Cor. 8:12). My declining strength permits me neither to lift nor to turn myself, and this is the only position I can stay in for talking to you. I hope to speak distinctly enough to be heard by all.

Consider the unusual situation of a man who for a number of months already (and perhaps for another unknown period of time) lives with the constant thought that his ties with life have been broken, that he is incurably and mortally stricken by God, and that he never knows at what moment the Father's voice will call him to his bosom. He would have to be either very insensitive or not at all reflective or very much deprived of all Christian feeling not to cast a backward glance over his past life. At the same time, thoughts of healing also arise, and must arise in his soul because, after all, he is in the hands of God, who raises the dead and has raised those more dead than he. Thus he is brought to ask himself, "If life were restored to me, what use would I make of it?"

While recalling the weakness and fragility of his resolves that a whole lifetime has demonstrated, he hopes, nevertheless, that through God's goodness such a visitation would not be lost for the second part of his career and ministry. Thus I say to myself, "Here is the sort of thing I would like to do," and certainly there is not a one that I would not like to do differently and better than I have done it in the past. There is a healthy humbling for me, just as there can be a healthy instruction for you, in considering these regrets of a man who is dying (or who believes himself to be dying) and who imagines the new use he would like to make of life if it were restored to him. It is especially along such lines that I propose to direct these talks.

If I could begin again, I would like to bring about a great change in my life, that is to say, my inner life. It goes without saying that there are intimate applications of the principle I just set forth that are the province of the Lord, but there are other more general applications that can appropriately be treated in a small gathering such as this. They are, for example, prayer, Bible reading, and Christian liberty.

In order to choose a specific example right away, here is one such point that strikes me. I regret having ruled my life too much according to my own plans—and by this I mean my own plans for Christian faithfulness and sanctification—and not enough simply according to the plan that the Lord opens up for each of us right before our eyes. I believe it will be easy for me in just a few words to explain my thoughts so that any child of God can enter into them right away.

Our Good Way

We are led to make for ourselves a certain ideal of the Christian life, Christian activity, and Christian ministry, and to attach certain plans and methods to that ideal in such a way that we are content only if we manage to achieve them. Thus it is important to make the best possible plans and to seek the best method to bring them about. All that is good, no doubt, but down at its foundation there is a flaw. It is the me, the hidden me that has rooted itself in the depths of the heart and that appears far too much in even the best and purest of our works. Rather than take the plan for my life and my daily conduct from my ideas and feelings, I would like to take them from the commandments of God, from his inner witnesses, from the guidance of his Spirit, and from the external directions he gives to our lives.

JESUS' BETTER WAY

You will understand perfectly my thinking on the way in which I would like to order my life if you consider the way in which Jesus ordered his life. In Jesus we do not find those plans and methods that have so much occupied so many good people, that have so often tormented them, and that have taken a considerable amount of time that they could have put to better use. But what do we find? We find a man—I here consider him as the Son of man—who intends nothing but to accomplish the mission he has received from the Father and who has no other plan than to enter into the Father's plan. Thus, with his eyes fixed upon the Father, he is concerned only with listening to his voice in order to follow it and with discerning his will in order to carry it out.

The good works of Jesus Christ are all given to him one at a time, each having been placed before him along his path by the hand of God. They follow each other so naturally, are born so easily one from another, that they never interfere with one another, even on the busiest days of his ministry. Consider, for example, the day that is described to us in the ninth chapter of Saint Matthew, where he calls one of the apostles, heals the sick, raises someone from the dead, and, in passing, delivers a woman who has been ill for a number of years, not to mention the other blessings he showers in all directions along his route. In all of this there is not a minute of hindrance or hesitation, either for the way to order his works or for the time to give to each one. This is because Jesus Christ very simply follows God's plan and because God has undertaken to guide him.

When there is this perfect harmony with the will of God, there is also, on God's part, a perfect clarity in directing us. Then we can see the living out of that wonderful and profound word of the Holy Spirit, "For we are . . . created in Christ Jesus to do good works, which God prepared in advance for us to do" (Eph. 2:10). Here good works are presented to us not as a way that we have to make for ourselves but as a way that God has made and in which we need only walk. It is God's path, not our own. We have only to follow it and we will, moment by moment, do the will of God.

If I have enabled you to understand (as much as I can with so little development) what I would like to have done and what I would wish to do if life were restored to me, then it will be easy to make you grasp the many advantages of this conformity to God's plan as opposed to following our personal plans, even the best of them. Let me add in passing that my aim is not to discourage personal plans. I believe that our infirmity has need of this crutch, and we must seek to make the best plans possible, provided that our personal plans are always subordinate to the general thought of following only the will of God.

A HOLY LIFE

Very well, to limit myself to two or three main ideas, that way of life exemplified by Jesus Christ is first of all a condition of holiness. What is it that constitutes sin in its very essence? It is self-seeking, self-confidence, self-will, self-righteousness, self-glory, and all that which relates to us personally. Therefore those desires to do good and even to do the will of the Lord that rely on plans and projects formed inside ourselves inevitably partake, in some sense, of the root of sin.

On the contrary, the essence of holiness is the union of our will with the divine will. When we shall have no other plan than God's plan and no other will than God's will, then we will be in a state of true holiness, a holiness that will not simply have an external appearance but that will have an internal character. We will be in a state of holiness similar to the holiness of Jesus Christ.

The holiness of Jesus Christ follows from and depends upon the principle I set forth just a moment ago: constant abandonment to the plain will of God, which is manifested on the inside by the witness of his Spirit and on the outside by the declarations of his Word and by the signs of his providence. Jesus Christ is holy because he wants only what God wants, because he does not seek his glory but that of the Father. That has been the power of his holiness. Thus this conformity to God's plan is, first of all, a condition of holiness.

AN ACTIVE LIFE

At the same time, it is a condition of activity. One loses an enormous amount of time finding his own way, even in the good things. He considers, with reason, how easy it would be to be mistaken and thus gives himself up to infinite reflections and considerations. How many men have recognized at the end of their careers that a considerable part of their lives was spent forming plans when it would have been better spent on the work of the present moment and in the interest of others!

See what activity is communicated to Jesus Christ through this plan of his that I just described to you. In the ninth chapter of Saint Matthew and elsewhere, the good works flow out unstintingly, not one on top of another but one after another. There is no limit to activity founded on that complete harmony with the will of God where man's action becomes a divine action and his life becomes like a divine life in the midst of humanity, having something of the power of God at work within it.

We have no idea of what we would be able to do if we were completely lost in such total harmony with God; if we would seek no other will than his. We have no idea of what we would be able to do if every word in our mouth, every beat of our heart, every thought of our minds, every movement of our spirit and body were oriented toward him to wait for him in the spirit of Samuel: "Speak, for your servant is listening" (1 Sam. 3:10). A few men—Luther, Calvin, Saint Paul, Moses—have demonstrated what a man can do when he seeks only the will of God. Jesus Christ has done much more because in him alone has the conformity of his will with the divine will been perfect. Such conformity is thus a condition of activity, and of almost limitless activity. Nevertheless, there are limits because God never asks of his creatures more than that of which they are capable.

A PEACEFUL LIFE

Finally, and I will end there, this way of life is a condition of peace. There is no peace for the man who takes his point of departure from within himself. There is always room to fear that he is mistaken. He is troubled and often in error because human will and interest are subject to many

135

errors. He has no rest. He is agitated and tormented. He inspires a deep compassion in the one who, while seeing his pure desire to glorify God, sees also the extent to which he himself has put obstacles in his path by his lack of simplicity. By contrast, when we look only to God, we cast all of our burdens onto him, and he will sustain us.

There is more. If my projects originate with me, they may not be possible. I would like to follow a career, but it would require expenditures that I am unable to provide. I would like to be a painter, and I lack eyesight; an orator, and I have no voice; a surgeon, and my hand shakes. There is my missed career over which I will never be able to console myself. But there will never be a missed career if my projects are taken from God's plan regarding me. Then even the impossibility where I am faced with doing the things I just proposed proves to me that they are not what God calls me to, and even the infirmities that stop me are like lights by which God reveals my true work to me. If we act in that spirit (I say it with deep respect) our work is God's affair rather than ours, his work and not ours. The activity, the personal action that God always requires of us consists only of following him in faithful, abandoned obedience. There we will find a deep peace. God cannot lead us astray.

Often we are agitated by the thought that we are not doing enough or that we are doing evil or that we are not doing the work that God has given us to do. I remember in particular how, during the first weeks following the doctors' declaration, I was troubled by the thought that my work was not done. By the grace of God I have been delivered from those thoughts, because I have understood that it is not a question of my work but of God's. I have recognized that even through the suffering and afflictions he has sent me and through the hope of the eternal life that must follow them, the Lord has me exercising a different ministry. It is probably more important than the one I had proposed for myself and is, in any case, more certain[1] because it comes to me more directly from the hand of God, who mercifully constrains me to walk in that path for his service and for his glory. It is by living with this mindset that we will be able to say, like the dying Jesus Christ, "I have finished the work which you have given me to do" (John 17:4 NKJV). Why could he say that? Because he seeks only to do the work of God, and God withdraws him like a ripe fruit when his mission is accomplished.

A COMPLETE LIFE

Very well then, let us too seek nothing but to do the work the Father has given us to do, and let us put ourselves back into his hands. We too, if we are faithful, will be withdrawn only when our work is finished. It is for God alone to decide when the work that he wants to do through us is accomplished. It might be quite imperfect, quite incomplete in men's eyes, but in the end, if we are right before him, the Lord will not permit our life to pass without leaving some mark upon the earth. He will not withdraw us until, in his eyes, our work is done. Then we will be able to say like the Lord in a spirit of humility, "I have finished the work which you have given me to do."

Vinet said it without knowing it when he gave his last theology lesson on these words, "I have finished the work

---

1 That is, more certain to be in the Lord's will and thus to accomplish his purposes.

which you have given me to do."[2] That which was accomplished in Vinet was accomplished also in Rochat and is being accomplished in all of God's servants. There is great peace in seeking our plan only in God and in following it while renouncing self. There is no peace except in that.

Therefore, let us apply ourselves to seeking our plan in God alone, both those who are called back to him, so that they may humble themselves, and those who are living, so that they may grow in grace. Let us apply ourselves in that spirit to follow Jesus Christ in his Gethsemane and to keep our eyes constantly fixed on the Father's will. This will be for us, as it was for Jesus Christ, a condition of holiness, a condition of activity, and a condition of deep peace. It is that peace that I desire for you.

I would be quite happy to think that these few reflections might have excited those who still have time, life, and strength before them to use them so faithfully, so simply to glorify God, following their Savior's example, that they might be able to say in their turn, "I have finished the work which you have given me to do." Then they could spend the rest of their earthly life in deep peace while waiting to be called back from this world to the Father, by the grace of the Lord, and by the virtue and the anointing of the Holy Spirit.

To read the talks in original
chronological order, go to
the next chapter.

2 Alexander Rodolphe Vinet and Auguste Louis Philippe Rochat (mentioned later) were prominent figures among French-speaking evangelicals of Monod's day. Vinet died in 1847 at about age 50, while Rochat died sometime before the third edition of *Meditations on the Story of Hezekiah* was published in 1850.

20

FEEDING ON GOD'S WORD

(January 20, 1856)

My son, pay attention to what I say;
    listen closely to my words.
Do not let them out of your sight,
    keep them within your heart;
for they are life to those who find them
    and health to a man's whole body.
Above all else, guard your heart,
    for it is the wellspring of life.

Proverbs 4:20–23

My dear friends, last Sunday under the theme *A Dying Man's Regrets* I began to explain the new perspective that one who is dying receives about the many things he would now like to have done differently and that he would like to do differently if he were called back from his half-open tomb. One of the most important of these is our study of God's Word. Ah, certainly in such a case one says to himself, "I should have acted differently with regard to the Word of God. I should have studied it more deeply and possessed it more fully so as to practice it better while communicating it more effectively to others!" Let us stop for a few brief moments on this healthy thought so that we may humble those for whom the end of time is coming and enlighten those to whom more time is given but who don't know for how long.

THE VALUE OF SCRIPTURE

What is Holy Scripture? Never will men be able to explain how it was formed or, in particular, how God's Spirit and man's spirit are combined there to make it a divine word, as high as the heavens, and yet, at the same time, a human word very close to us. This is no less difficult to explain than how in Jesus Christ the divine and human natures are united. This comparison does not come from me but from Scripture, which calls itself the written Word and Jesus Christ the living Word.

No matter how it was formed, Holy Scripture is heaven spoken on earth. It is the maxims of the kingdom of heaven that are communicated to men in a human language. It is as if the invisible kingdom had descended into their midst and been placed before their eyes. There is no other book, even among the best, that communicates the mysteries of the kingdom of heaven to us as this one does. They are all mixed with human error; only Scripture is exempt from it. It is God's book filled with God's truth. In it we hear God speaking through the Holy Spirit; we see God, man, the present, the future, time, and eternity described such as they are.

INTERROGATING SCRIPTURE

If someone has thus taken account of what Scripture is, it will not be hard for him to confess the use to which he should put it. We should interrogate Scripture just as we would like to interrogate an angel from heaven sent expressly by God at this very moment in order to instruct us. Or, what is even better, we should interrogate it as we would interrogate our Lord Jesus Christ if we had him near to us right now and could speak to him and hear him. In effect, we really do speak to him and hear him when we read Holy Scripture, and as it reveals him to us, it reveals everything else to us through his Spirit and on his behalf.

Oh, how can we surround this book with enough attention and respect? No doubt Scripture is not the truth that saves us, but it is the road to that truth. It is not salvation, but it is the book that reveals our salvation, a salvation we would never be able to know without it. Through Scripture and in proportion to our growth in understanding it, we will also become better acquainted with Jesus, the Savior of our souls.

No Christian will argue the truth of these principles, and yet those who study the Scriptures in depth are rare indeed! Most read them superficially and content themselves with a few great general truths when they could be probing ever deeper and becoming aware (as much as they can) of all that is there, as it is written: "The secret things belong to the LORD our God, but the things revealed belong to us and to our children forever" (Deut. 29:29). Why is there this singular contradiction within ourselves? It is because of the difficulties that such a reading presents.

OVERCOMING DIFFICULTIES

We must agree that when one begins to read Scripture in depth, he finds many difficulties and obscurities. Since it takes a lot of work to dissipate them and since man's spirit is naturally lazy and lax, little by little he loses courage and contents himself with reading and rereading Scripture always at the same level. This study scarcely penetrates below the surface and teaches nothing new. Rather, by always recapturing the same things, it even sometimes inspires in us a sort of weariness, as if the Word of God were not interesting, as if it were not able ever and always to instruct us, as if it were not as inexhaustible as God himself!

Nevertheless let us guard ourselves against thinking that these difficulties are insurmountable. No, my friends, but it takes effort, and here, as in prayer and in all the other aspects of the Christian life, God desires that man might be a co-laborer with him. Knowledge of the Bible, the flavor of the Bible, is the fruit and the reward of this humble and sincere and persevering effort.

Ah, that each one might return to his Bible with a new zeal! Take book after book, seeking to gain from reading it not simply general feelings of obvious piety but a thorough and growing acquaintance with the kingdom of heaven. Study a book until you have understood it as well as you can. Then go on to a second, then to a third, and so on. You will find that on a second and third reading many of the seemingly insurmountable difficulties will disappear, and even when some remain, you will nevertheless gain the fruit of your labor before God.

Do not exempt from this study even the most difficult books, the prophets, the minor prophets, which many Christians leave aside as unintelligible. If you want to make the effort to study them, you will see a multitude of very interesting things there. Besides, there are by God's grace good books and commentaries on certain parts of Scripture that can serve as a key for the others. In availing ourselves of these good books, we probe ever deeper in the knowledge of God's Word. Then we can apply ourselves more particularly to those parts of Scripture that address themselves more specifically to Christians, but, I repeat, without neglecting any of them.

THE FRUIT OF OUR LABORS

The fruit and the reward of those who are faithful and persevering will be to understand the Word of God, to love it, to penetrate ever further into it, and to find the time ever too short to know it well. I knew a man who spent seven hours each day studying the Bible and who found ever-increasing delights through that study.

If someone, in faith, using the resources God has placed at his disposal and counting on God to guide him, acted on these thoughts that I can only indicate briefly at this time, he would find as yet unsuspected treasures in God's Word. Thus it would become for him just as firm a support as it was for Jesus tempted in the wilderness. It would become for him what it was for the saints of the New Testament and of the Old Testament (with the portions of Scripture that existed before them); what it was for David and for Daniel, what it was for Saint Paul, what it was for all the saints of God.

May God grant each of us this grace! And may he for whom it is no more difficult to bless in a short time than in a long one, nor to bless one with little strength than one with much, be pleased to make these words of mine so penetrate into your hearts that they will work a transformation in your study of the Bible, a transformation for which you will bless God through all eternity! Amen.

To read the talks in original
chronological order, go to
the next chapter.

21

THE USE OF TIME

(January 27, 1856)

Be very careful, then, how you live—not as unwise but as wise, making the most of every opportunity, because the days are evil. Therefore do not be foolish, but understand what the Lord's will is. Do not get drunk on wine, which leads to debauchery. Instead, be filled with the Spirit.

Ephesians 5:15–18

My strength is used up, my dear friends, and I was asking myself if I should not keep silent this week. I will, however, say what I intended to say to you, while limiting myself simply to indicating my thoughts.

One of the things that troubles a Christian who believes he is reaching the end of his life (or that would trouble him if it were not at the foot of the cross) is the way in which he has used his time. As a result, it is the subject of one of the exhortations he must address to his living brothers.

SEIZING OPPORTUNITIES

It is written, "redeem the opportunity," which is a better version than the one that reads "redeem the time" (see
Eph. 5:16 KJV). To redeem or buy back does not mean to
buy for a second time but to buy eagerly. Eagerly buy the
opportunity God furnishes you, for the days are evil, so that
once an opportunity is missed, it can never return. The
good use of time is, in itself, such a grand idea that it fright-
ens the soul. There is something more modest in the
thought: eagerly seize the opportunities God furnishes you
as he brings them into being. How much time and how
many opportunities are lost through laziness, through unbelief, through carelessness, through self-centeredness,
through self-will, through indecision, through attachment
to sin, and through a thousand other things! It is hardly
necessary to belabor this point, for there is not a Christian
whose heart does not condemn him and whose conscience
is not gripped by it.

Ah, how precious and sufficient is the time that God
gives us! God, who is just, measures out the time with the
work and the work with the time, never giving us a good
work to do for which the time is lacking or a single moment
of our lives where we do not have some good thing to do.
But how to arrive at thus filling all of our time? How to succeed in doing at least some part of the enormous good that
a single man could accomplish if he put into practice the
precept: "All that you have the means to do, do it according
to your ability," and if he were constantly busy serving the
Lord? I would like to give you two or three indications of
how to accomplish this and then leave to your conscience
the job of developing them.

OUR TIME BELONGS TO GOD

First, we must be filled with the thought that we do not belong to ourselves and that our time does not belong to us any more than anything else does. Our time is God's, and, as a result, it is in God that we must always seek what we should do to fill the time he gives us. It is in God that we must seek to respond to the opportunities with which he presents us. I assure you that illness gives some very precious lessons on the subject—that is to say, on our belonging not to ourselves but to God.

Our heart is naturally prone—and this is the very root of sin—to consider itself the center and aim of life. But when one is ill, when one suffers, how could he find comfort if he sought the purpose of his life within himself? The purpose of life in such a case is totally missing. Illness teaches us that it is necessary to look for life's goal elsewhere; that we live not to be happy on earth but rather to glorify God, something we can do in sickness as well as in health, and often better. Therefore let us learn from sickness, from all of life's sufferings, and from the whole Word of God that our time belongs to God and that for us it is only a question of using it for his glory.

BE EAGER

Second, let us always be eager to seize the opportunities God gives us—they will in no wise be lacking—and we will find before us a life completely woven together of good works, fully prepared, in which we need only to walk. These works will link themselves together, with one begetting another so easily that our life will be nothing but good work, obedience, and, as a result (as we have mentioned earlier),

147

joy and peace in the Holy Spirit. For this to happen, we need eyes constantly opened and turned toward God, saying to him, "Lord, here I am. What do you want me to do?" and once it is done, "Lord, what do you want me to do now?" This leaves no interval that is not filled with the obedience due to God. In the same measure, God will then provide us with the opportunity to do an inexpressible amount of good. It is impossible to calculate the good that could enter into the life of one single man so disposed; witness the man Jesus Christ.

In the things of this world, the men who have done the most are the men who have lived by this principle of seizing opportunities. If you study carefully the lives of men who have done very extended and numerous works—such as Calvin or Luther or Bossuet—you will recognize that they did the things that presented themselves and to the extent that they presented themselves along their paths. You will see that these are men who were called very gently by circumstances to do what they did. Bossuet was led by the educational needs of the crown prince to compose his best works. Calvin and Luther did their best writing in response to circumstances.

By contrast, ordinary men who do little are those who do not know how to seize opportunity in order to profit from it. They could, perhaps, have done just as much as the men who did much, but they lacked the art of seizing opportunities. And the true art of seizing opportunities is the Christian art of having our eyes ever turned toward the Lord, of taking each work as he presents it to us, and, when it is done, of passing on to another. It is amazing what one human life can accomplish in this way, simply by following the path that the Lord clearly opens up before each one of us.

BE ORDERLY

Third, it is necessary to act with order and method, ⑦
never leaving to chance the use of the time that God gives
us. Some days ago I said that we should not make our own
plans, but it is not a contradiction to say that we should act
systematically, provided that the system is taken in the Lord.
In order to do the things God gives us to do, we must bring
order and method to bear. Thus it is appropriate that we
have set hours for awakening and for our work; that, as
much as possible, we be men who are exact in the hours of
our meals and all of our other varied activities. In this way
life is much simpler, smoother, easier to fill. It is like a ready-
made framework upon which the Lord has only to build.

The men who have done the most are the men who have
known how to order their lives calmly and forcefully, especially if they were able to combine that firmness with a live-
liness of spirit, a warmth of soul. These traits do not always
go with a spirit of order and method but, when combined
with it, enable a man to do the most astounding things. It is
said that the philosopher Kant sometimes amused himself
by summoning his servant and having him testify to the fact
that for forty years he had gotten up every day at four o'-
clock! Just imagine how much someone who gets up at four
o'clock every morning can do!

Note, by the way, the power of this method, independent
of the hour for arising. By the mere fact of having a set hour
for getting up, how much more time one has to devote to the
Lord, simply because if I get up every day at a fixed hour, I
have regulated that hour, with prayer, before God, taking account of Christian common sense and wisdom. On the contrary, if I get up at random, then the hour at which I do so

is governed by the impulse of the moment—that is to say, by all kinds of circumstances over which I should be able to triumph. It will be governed by laziness, by the desire for "a little sleep, a little slumber, a little folding of the hands to rest—and poverty will come on you like a bandit" (Prov. 6:10–11); not simply poverty of money, but of spirit, of work, and of service for God.

Thus method—a life peacefully ordered before the Lord—is something of the highest importance in learning to do much for God's service.

Be Prudent

Finally, in order not to multiply my thoughts, let us keep our bodies and spirits in a disposition that brings no hindrance to this good use of the time and gifts that we have received to be used according to God's desire. Sadness, uneven tempers, the bent toward self-will, the seeking after self, the desire for the glory that comes from men are all obstacles that surround and harass us ceaselessly, and we must apply ourselves diligently to gain the victory over them.

And the body, let us not neglect it. Poor health, a weak body, is often a great obstacle to accomplishing our work before God. We must accept it when God sends it, but it is our duty before him to take the exercise necessary for the body and to use the needed precautions to strengthen it for the service and the glory of God (that thought which raises and sanctifies everything). There are many men who would have been able to do much more than they did for the glory of God if they had not given themselves over to an activity that was more pious than considered and that exhausted them while they were still young. Those who die early need to examine whether they should not reproach themselves in this area. They need to determine whether they have neglected certain simple, easy precautions in which it is hard to persevere but that would have allowed them to work a longer time in the service of God.

But before all else, let us fortify the spirit and soul, and let us avoid everything that could hinder the action God wants to accomplish in us and through us.

THE REWARD

My friends, not one of us knows how much more time God has left for us, but we know the time that he has already given us and how much we need to reproach ourselves for the use we have made of it. Let us seize that which remains ahead of us, strong or weak, healthy or sick, living or dying. We have a Savior who always filled each moment with obedience to God. Let us walk in his footsteps, toward glory through the cross, and in the end we will hear that sweet voice: "Well done, good and faithful servant! You have been faithful with a few things; I will put you in charge of many things" (Matt. 25:21).

To read the talks in original
chronological order, go to
the next chapter.

Consistent, Fervent Prayer

(February 3, 1856)

This is what the LORD says: "When seventy years are completed for Babylon, I will come to you and fulfill my gracious promise to bring you back to this place. For I know the plans I have for you," declares the LORD, "plans to prosper you and not to harm you, plans to give you hope and a future. Then you will call upon me and come and pray to me, and I will listen to you. You will seek me and find me when you seek me with all your heart. I will be found by you," declares the LORD, "and will bring you back from captivity."

Jeremiah 29:10–14

My dear friends in Christ, among the subjects about which a Christian who believes himself to be near his end carries regrets, there is certainly none he would want so much to reform, if he returned to life, as prayer.

THE WEAKNESS OF OUR PRAYER

What does prayer really amount to for most Christians (that is, for believing Christians who pray)? A few moments in the morning devoted to quiet meditation, a few moments in the evening—longer or shorter and sometimes very short. Then, in extraordinary circumstances, when a special need to approach him is felt, the heart lifts itself up to God. It is to these meager proportions that the habits of many Christians (or men who call themselves by that name) are reduced.

In addition, how little the majority of professing Christians know of the fruit of prayer promised in Scripture! Where is the powerful fruit of sanctification that causes the soul to triumph over every temptation as Jesus did in the desert and that makes it more than victorious in him who loved us? Where is the fruit of consolation that pours a sweet, deep joy into the soul; a joy capable of overcoming all the afflictions of earth? Even in anguish and bitterness, whether of spirit and heart or of the flesh, the soul that has this consolation is still able to rejoice with that perfect joy the dying Jesus wished for his disciples—disciples who would, themselves, lead lives full of dying.[1] Where is that fruit of deliverance in which the soul obtains from God all that it asks? It matters not whether it says with Jesus, "I knew that you always hear me" (John 11:42) or whether, rather

---

1 Lives full of death to self and a willingness to suffer for the sake of the gospel.

than lift itself so high, it can at least say with David, "You are accustomed to hearing me."[2]

Let us be honest and recognize that there is an enormous distance between the promises of Scripture made in regard to prayer and the fruit we gather from it. More than once our feeble faith has been troubled or perhaps momentarily shaken by this fact, and we have said to ourselves, "Is that all?" No, that is not all that was promised, but then we have not done all that was commanded. Ah, my friends, prayer as I have just painted it from life is very different from prayer as Scripture presents it; very different from the prayer to which the promises are made!

SCRIPTURAL PRAYER

What is prayer according to Scripture? Some days ago I said that Holy Scripture, the Word of God, is heaven speaking. In pursuing that same image, I would say that scriptural prayer is heaven received inside of us by the Holy Spirit. Without the Word, prayer is nothing, having no source of nourishment. Without prayer, the Word is powerless and does not penetrate into the heart. But when the truths of heaven that completely fill Scripture are received and assimilated by the very substance of our souls through prayer, when they penetrate to the very core of our inner man, then

2 The specific Scripture reference here is unclear. Perhaps it is to Psalm 120:1, which the King James Version renders in the past tense but which French Bibles and other English translations give in a continuing present ("I call on the Lord in my distress, and he answers me.") The verb used in the Hebrew and the French has the dual sense of hearing (paying attention to) and responding, though responding or granting is the dominant thought in the French.

we know that prayer causes heaven and all its benefits, the Holy Spirit and all his gifts, God and all his promises to enter into us.

Prayer is the key that God has placed in our hands to put us in communication with the invisible world. Everything through prayer; nothing without it. I say the key that God has placed in *our* hands, because there is another that he has kept in his own. Now and then he will deign to use it to open the invisible world to us when we have neglected to open it ourselves; when we have failed to put ourselves in harmony with him and cooperate with his divine work as "God's fellow workers" (1 Cor. 3:9). Thus, in striking down Saul on the road to Damascus and raising him up a different man, God opened heaven to him even while Saul, far from seeking it, was seeking Christ's disciples in order to torture them and have them killed. But these are those strokes of grace on which we must not rely and that are all the less likely to be granted to us the more we count on them.

No doubt, at the bottom of even these acts of grace we would still find, if we think about it carefully, a soul sincerely seeking God. This same Saul of Tarsus who was going around persecuting the name of Jesus in his followers had nevertheless a sincere heart that was searching for God and demanding the truth from him. Perhaps from the time that Saint Stephen prayed for those who caused his death, the spark of a new life had begun to penetrate into Saul's soul. How can we know?

Whatever the case, God's usual way is to grant these graces in response to prayer and to wait for prayer before granting them. As Isaiah says, "Therefore will the LORD wait, that he may be gracious unto you" (Isa. 30:18 KJV).

What is he waiting for? He is waiting for you to cry out to him. And in Jeremiah it says, "Then you will call upon me and come and pray to me, and I will listen to you. You will seek me and find me when you seek me with all your heart" (Jer. 29:12–13). It is the same for us. It is through prayer that we can obtain all. It is to true prayer as Scripture depicts it for us that all the promises are made.

THE PRAYERS OF GOD'S SERVANTS

Also, my friends, prayer is the distinctive mark of the Lord's powerful servants. All of them, in spite of considerable differences, offer us this common trait: they are men who pray much and men who pray fervently.

Look at the prayers of Jacob. He battles God for an entire night until he has triumphed over the Lord himself, who allows this victory in order to exercise the faith of his servant. Look at the prayers of Moses and of Samuel; Moses, the founder of Israel, and Samuel, its reformer. Jeremiah said of them in the beginning of his fifteenth chapter, in order to show that God had resolved not to grant mercy in a certain situation: "Even if Moses and Samuel were to stand before me, my heart would not go out to this people" (Jer. 15:1). Suppose we tried to substitute our names for those of Moses or Samuel. "Though this or that one among us had prayed, still it would not be granted." What a comedown! What humiliation! What nonsense!

Look at the prayers of David, the psalms, those prayers that were able not only to support David but that are like 150 pillars supporting all the people of God from generation to generation and that will keep on supporting them until the end of the world.

Look at the prayers of King Jehoshaphat, who through prayer alone destroys the combined armies of the Moabites, the Ammonites, and the inhabitants of Mount Seir (see 2 Chron. 20). And look at the prayers of King Hezekiah, his direct descendent[3] and imitator. Through prayer alone he calls forth the extermination of the avenging God on an army of 185,000 men who are only waiting for an opportunity to destroy Jerusalem completely (see 2 Kings 18–19). Look at the prayers of Ezra and Nehemiah for the reestablishment and reformation of their people according to the example of Moses and Samuel; one restoring the spiritual state and the observance of the law, the other rebuilding the walls of Jerusalem and reestablishing civil order.

Look at the prayers of Jesus, "the author and finisher of our faith." Though he is fully Jesus, fully the Son of God, he prays; he spends whole nights in prayer and does nothing except through prayer. Through prayer he names the group of apostles. Through prayer he sustains the apostles. Through prayer he triumphs over the devil in the desert, in Gethsemane, and on Golgotha. Through prayer he accomplishes the complete work of our redemption, having been enabled to suffer unheard-of pains. Our most awful sufferings can just barely let us glimpse a pale image of what he endured.

And following Jesus, see the series of men of prayer begin again. Look at Paul, what a giant of prayer! Prayer is the soul and the strength of all his work. Paul is Paul, above all, through prayer.

---

3 The literal "great-grandson" is used here in a more generic sense, since Hezekiah is a much later descendent of Jehoshaphat.

Look at the prayers of Saint Augustine, the prayers of Calvin. Look at the prayers of Luther, who, during the time that he was appearing before the Diet of Worms, spent three hours taken from the best part of the day crying aloud to God, not knowing that his faithful friend Dietrich was lending an indiscreet ear and assembling those prayers of fire for the good of the church.[4] Look at the prayers of Pascal. While still quite young he was visited by cruel and constant pain but was enabled to overcome it with a strength and piety of which we find the deep, indelible mark in his prayers—such lovely, strong prayers that have been preserved for us.

Behold the prayers of all the saints of all ages. It is their faith, their life, their strength, their work.

4 Here is what Dietrich wrote to Melancthon (*Schreiben an Ph. Melancthon*, Walch, Teil 14:2139) in speaking of Luther's stay at Coburg during the Diet of Augsburg: "I cannot sufficiently admire his resolve, his joy, his faith, and his hope in these times of desolation. He strengthens himself each day in these feelings through constant application to the Word of God. There is not a single day in which he does not reserve *at least three hours* for prayer, taken from the time during the day that is most conducive to work. One day I had the privilege of hearing him pray. Great God, what spirit, what faith in his words! He prays with all of the reserve of a man who is before God, but with all of the confidence of a child speaking to his father. 'I know,' he said, 'that you are our good God and our Father; that is why I am persuaded that you will exterminate those who persecute your children. If you don't do it, the risk for you is as great as it is for us. This is your cause; and what we have done we were unable to leave undone. It is up to you, merciful Father, to protect us.' As I listened from a distance to him praying these words in a clear voice, my heart burned with joy within me, because I was hearing him speak to God with so much fervor and with complete liberty. Above all, he leaned so firmly on the promises of Psalms that he seemed assured that nothing which he asked could fail to be accomplished." [This footnote was translated from the French.]

GOD, TEACH US TO PRAY

Oh, my friends, I don't know whether you will be as deeply humbled by these recollections as I am. For myself, I cannot express just how much I am humbled in remembering what my prayers have been, compared with what they should have been and could have been. Certainly we would be, in our humble sphere of action, what these men were in the history of Scripture and of the church, if only we knew how to pray as they knew how to pray; if instead of saying "God gave them a special privilege," we but knew to say, "Lord, teach me to pray."

Ah, if I were restored to life, I would like, with God's help and in spite of myself, to give prayer much more time than I have done and to lean on prayer much more than on work. It is our duty never to neglect work, but work has no strength except when supported and animated by prayer. Above all, I would like to pour into my prayers that anointing and fervor of the Holy Spirit that are not learned in a day but are the fruit of a long and often painful apprenticeship.

Oh, my friends, you who are full of life, you whose careers do not yet seem to be reaching their end (though we know nothing about it, and I could live longer than you), seize the opportunity and redeem it! Begin new habits of prayer. Bring to prayer not only a spirit of fervor, but also a spirit of order and method that will increase its power as it increases the power of all human affairs, assisting divine power itself. This is the order and method that Jesus gave us in the model prayer, the Lord's Prayer. Finally, ask God to guide you, and leave here full of this prayer: "Lord, teach me to pray!" I will apply myself to do the same along with you, however short my time may be. God does not look at the shortness of the time but at the uprightness of the heart.

All together, with one spirit and one heart, humbled by the slackness of our prayers, let us form the holy resolve finally to know through experience the true promises of prayer so that we might harvest from it the blessed heritage of the invisible world. Only prayer can put us in contact with the invisible world through the Word of God. That world is closer to some and further from others than they either think or desire. In any case, whether in ten years or in twenty or fifty, or even a hundred years, which would be enormous (that is to say, in the blink of an eye), this invisible world will open itself to all of us who have put their full hope in Jesus Christ crucified and resurrected from the dead.

This is my ardent prayer for you, and, if the Lord calls me back to himself, this is the heritage I would like to leave to each one of you, beginning with my beloved family! Amen.

To read the talks in original
chronological order, go to
the next chapter.

FOCUSING ON THE IMPORTANT

(February 10, 1856)

Therefore, since we are surrounded by such a great
cloud of witnesses, let us throw off everything that
hinders and the sin that so easily entangles, and let
us run with perseverance the race marked out for us.
Let us fix our eyes on Jesus, the author and perfecter
of our faith, who for the joy set before him endured
the cross, scorning its shame, and sat down at the
right hand of the throne of God.

Hebrews 12:1–2

My beloved friends, who demonstrate your brotherly
love to me by once again joining me to share in the Lord's
love feast, there are things that would trouble the soul of a
man facing death if that soul were not reassured about
them—as about all things—by the totally free grace of God

161

in Jesus Christ. One of those things is the memory of that part of his life that was lost, or more than lost, on minor matters rather than being spent on the great matters that alone should be constantly before the eyes of a Christian. That is why I would like to take a moment to call your attention to the great harm that is done when a Christian is preoccupied with minor matters.[1]

WHAT MAKES THINGS IMPORTANT?

Let us be clear right at the beginning that preoccupation with minor matters is not to be confused with attention given to little things. We are called by God to be involved with a whole host of little things, and indeed they make up much of life. The way in which we fulfill the small duties is just as true a measure of our piety as the way in which we fulfill our great duties. Often it is an even truer measure, because in the small things we have only God, ourselves, and our family as witnesses, while in accomplishing the great ones we are placed in a sort of theater where our pride sometimes finds itself only too willing to be set up.

Besides, nothing is small or great in itself. It becomes so only by the spirit we bring to it. Before God, since he is infinite and eternal, what we call small is just as great as what we call the greatest of all, and that which we call great is just as small as what we call the smallest of all. A faithful maidservant who, for the love of God, takes affectionate care of a

---

1 The word translated "minor" is the common French word *petit*, which normally means "small" but also can signify "petty" or "of little importance." The same word is translated "little" in the next paragraph, where Monod contrasts *petits intérêts* ("minor matters") with *petites choses* ("little things" or "details").

child confided to her by her masters does a great thing before God, and she shall have her reward. But a statesman who, through self-love, aspires to the highest honors for wisdom or eloquence does a very small thing before God and may draw more shame upon himself in heaven than glory on earth.

What is important, then, is to approach everything we do with a great, exalted spirit that always looks toward God and that does all things in light of him and of eternity. Thus, by carrying God everywhere in our hearts, we would also carry him everywhere in our words and in our work, so that there might be nothing petty or earthly or transitory in our entire lives.

WHAT IS IMPORTANT TO GOD?

The example of God himself will suffice to clarify for us what I have just said. God makes no difference in the care he brings to the little things as opposed to the big ones. He constructs a blade of grass or a snowflake with as much care as he determines the proportions, the relations, and the movements of the stars. Whether he builds a grain of sand or establishes a Mont Blanc, he does everything he does as God—that is, with perfect care. But this God who sees nothing as too small to merit his attention always has, in his small works as well as in his large ones, eternity, his reign, and his glory before his eyes, just as he has said: "The LORD does all things for his glory" (apparently a reference to Prov. 16:4). There is absolutely nothing in all of God's works, whether moral or physical, to which he has not brought the immense weight of an infinite care and an eternal interest.

It is the same with Jesus, God made visible. Certainly he

doesn't neglect the poor little children who are brought to him and whom the apostles thought it beneath him to bless. Beyond that, he doesn't even neglect the leftover fragments of bread and fish. He wants nothing to be lost, even at a time when he has just demonstrated that with (or even without) a word he can multiply the bread and fishes at will. And this same Jesus is the one who accomplishes the greatest works in his incarnation, his redemption, his passion, his resurrection, and his glorious ascension.

But he does all these things in the same spirit. Whether he is being made incarnate, redeeming us, suffering for us, rising from the dead, or ascending to the heavens; whether he is stopping to bless the little children, gathering the bits of bread and fish, speaking the smallest word of comfort to someone in affliction, or offering a cup of cold water to someone who is thirsty; always in each of these actions, he has God, eternity, and his Father's glory in view. Thus, in all of his works, Jesus Christ appears to us as having his head always in heaven while his feet are on the earth. He appears to us saying "the one who is in heaven" while speaking of himself. As everything is great within his soul, so too everything is great in all his works and in all his thoughts.

What Is Our Focus?

Very well, my dear friends. There is the example that is offered to us, and thus we must walk. We must not be preoccupied with the minor matters of earth, and still less with its lusts and sins. Rather we must always be preoccupied with God, with his glory, with his love, and with the work of Jesus Christ for the honor of God and the salvation of mankind, including our own. Made in the image and likeness of God, we must be his imitators. In the smallest cares as well as in the greatest, we must carry thoughts of God and of eternity always as our mindset. The Christian, whatever he says, whatever he does, must always be great before God, who weighs true greatness.

Painters have depicted the saints with a halo. Scripture does nothing of the sort except for one Old Testament saint.[2] Rather, it depicts them in a most exceptional way: the saints carry their halos inside of them and radiate the glow wherever they pass by.

It is necessary for the Christian to give such an impression of himself that no matter where one meets him—whether in the street, in the drawing room, at the dining table, in prison, or at the height of greatness—one should always have the feeling that this is a man who seeks God, who dreams of furthering the great interests of humanity, and who finds that it is not worth living for anything except to glorify God. He should always appear as one who makes all of his advantages and all of his misfortunes work together to that end, who is ready to leave this earth as soon as that work is accomplished, and who, like his Master, goes about from place to place doing good.

Oh, how holy and how happy this Christian would be, free from covetousness, envy, worry, and all that troubles the soul! By walking always with God, how he would bring honor to the gospel, how he would victoriously shut the mouth of scoffers, how many souls he would lead to his Savior, and all through the humble glow of a completely holy life even more than by his most powerful words!

2 Moses, whose face glowed when he had been talking with God.

AVOIDING DISTRACTIONS

But where are these Christians, my God? Where are they? How much easier it would be to find Christians, real Christians, who are sincere, who on dying would give their souls back into the Lord's hands, who deep down are longing for him, but who allow themselves to be turned aside and become preoccupied with the minor matters of life. They are absorbed by the love of money, by the thirst for the glory of man, by jealousy of a competitor's success, by an ardent desire for personal success, by an ambition outside of the paths God has marked out for them, by impatience with sickness, by an aversion to humiliations and crosses, by the lively annoyance they can experience over a word—perhaps a misunderstood word—or an insignificant mishap that will leave no trace of its presence at death or perhaps even in an hour!

Oh, my God, how few in number are the consistent Christians! That is why, my friends, the gospel is compromised by those who profess it. That is why one so often says of them that in the end they seek after just what everyone else seeks after and that the things that trouble others trouble them just as much. Thus the gospel is wounded even by those who seek their peace and salvation in it, those who should be using all of their strength and all of their life to glorify it. They should be walking with their heads high and in heaven, as Jesus did. They should be moving forward with their feet on the ground but breathing in the atmosphere of heaven, drawing from it the basis for all their actions and the strength for their entire life.

If only you knew, my friends, the extent to which all these illusions disappear when one looks death in the face.

166

How small these minor matters seem and how much only that which is great before God really appears great. How much one regrets not having lived more for God the way Jesus lived. How much, if one could begin life over again, one would like to lead it in a more serious way, more filled with Jesus Christ, with his Word and with his example.

If only you knew, you would put your hand to this work even this very moment! You would beseech God to put your conduct into harmony with your feelings and your faith. And you would succeed in this as many others have, after all, succeeded, because they cried out to God and because they *desired* it wholeheartedly before him. There is only a small handful of God's children gathered in this room around this bed of sickness and, most likely, death. Yet these Christians, with all their infirmities and weaknesses, would do more to advance God's rule and more for the good of humanity than a dense crowd armed with all possible gifts. They would do things that were that much greater because all thought of vain glory would ever more be banished far from their hearts.

This is my desire for you, my ardent prayer, and also the prayer I beg you to offer to God on my behalf, so that during my remaining time, whatever it might be, I would no longer dream of anything but to live for God's glory and the good of my fellows. This, of course, would also be to live for my own eternal joy! Amen.

To read the talks in original
chronological order, go to
chapt. 3 on p. 18.

part 6

REACHING THE GOAL

O the deep, deep love of Jesus,
Love of every loves the best!
'Tis an ocean vast of blessing,
'Tis a haven sweet of rest.
O the deep, deep love of Jesus,
'Tis a heav'n of heav'ns to me;
And it lifts me up to glory,
For it lifts me up to thee!

Samuel Trevor Francis
1834–1925

On Easter Sunday, two weeks before his death, when he surely must have sensed that his strength was nearly gone, Adolphe Monod's thoughts naturally turned toward Jesus' resurrection as foreshadowing our own. Then, at the very end of his life, his sole desire was to pour out his gratitude and praise for the deep, deep love of Jesus, thus bringing glory to God one last time.

RISEN WITH CHRIST

(March 23, 1856, Easter)

As for you, you were dead in your transgressions and sins, in which you used to live when you followed the ways of this world and of the ruler of the kingdom of the air, the spirit who is now at work in those who are disobedient. All of us also lived among them at one time, gratifying the cravings of our sinful nature and following its desires and thoughts. Like the rest, we were by nature objects of wrath. But because of his great love for us, God, who is rich in mercy, made us alive with Christ even when we were dead in trans-gressions—it is by grace you have been saved. And God raised us up with Christ and seated us with him in the heavenly realms in Christ Jesus, in order that in the coming ages he might show the incomparable riches of his grace, expressed in his kindness for us in Christ Jesus. For it is by grace you have been saved, through faith—and this not from yourselves, it is the gift of God—not by works, so that no one can boast. For we are God's workmanship, created in Christ Jesus to do good works, which God prepared in advance for us to do.

Ephesians 2:1–10

It is written, "Now faith is the substance of things hoped for, the evidence of things not seen" (Heb. 11:1 KJV); that is, it possesses that double virtue of making future things present and invisible things visible. Now, if there were an event in which this double virtue of faith were found to be realized and even incorporated, an event that adds the brightness of reality to the power of faith, would it not form the very foundation of all our enlightenment and the firmest support of our hope? This event is the resurrection of our Lord Jesus Christ.

THE INVISIBLE MADE VISIBLE

Scripture begins by so fully uniting the Christian to his Savior through faith that what happens to him happens to us, and his story is reproduced inwardly but truly in each of his children. If he dies, we die. If he is resurrected, we are resurrected. If he ascends to heaven, we ascend there too. This is how we are saved, because we are made one with Christ through faith. We are not allowed to seek him except in life and eternal glory, which obliges us to seek ourselves there also, we who are one with him through faith.

But see how Jesus Christ, having lived and died before the eyes of men, is also resurrected before their eyes and shows himself again to men after his resurrection. This means that the resurrection of Jesus Christ, which like everything else belongs to us, becomes a visible event, making our own resurrection visible, though previously it was invisible. You remember those heretics of whom Saint Paul speaks, who, considering the resurrection to be something purely spiritual, said that it had already happened. They are in flagrant opposition to the doctrine of the gospel, which makes the resurrection of our Lord and the one that we are to enjoy after him and with him a real, material, bodily fact. The gospel already visibly displays our resurrection in the resurrection of our Savior.

What an immense blessing and privilege it is for the Christian to contemplate in Jesus Christ visibly resurrected his own resurrection! His own seems to be invisible and in a sense really is so, but it becomes visible in his Savior. It is thus elevated above, let me not say doubts, but even difficulties of faith. It becomes an obvious, palpable fact that we find in Jesus Christ and that we apply to ourselves.

THE FUTURE MADE PRESENT

At the same time (for in my present state I can only sketch out my thoughts), the resurrection of the Lord Jesus Christ transforms a future event into a present and even a past event. If he had not been raised from the dead, we would always ponder the resurrection as something to come and thus always having an element of the obscure and intangible, even though the promises of God are certain in themselves. But here God has linked the promise to a historical fact. Jesus Christ has risen from the dead—there he is, he has been seen—and our resurrection, which is united with that of the Lord and which depends upon it, thus becomes itself a historical fact, a present fact, a past fact. That is why Saint Paul says, "We have already been resurrected" (see Eph. 2:5–6). Thus, by the resurrection of our Savior, our salvation is transformed from invisible to visible, from future to present. What more could we ask?

OUR ASSURANCE OF SALVATION

There is none but the Christian who can thus possess a firm assurance of his reconciliation with God and of his eternal happiness, because the invisible things have passed into the domain of the visible and present. He rejoices in contemplating them, as it were, before his eyes, and even now laying hold of them.

Also, you will note, my dear friends, that wherever the resurrection of our Savior is placed in the shadow, the assurance of our salvation is as well. Thus, in the Roman church, where attention is constantly called to the death of our Lord Jesus Christ and not to his resurrection and where the main, essential ceremony of the church, the Mass, is the celebration of the death of Jesus Christ, there is no assurance of salvation. One would even have qualms of conscience at being sure of his salvation, as if it were a kind of pride. Also, certain passages of Scripture are twisted to say that it is never permitted to be sure of one's salvation, so that there is never any peace, never any firm hope for the Christian.

Unfortunately, there are many Protestants who are no further advanced and who cannot rejoice in the assurance of their salvation. This comes from their failure to contemplate Jesus Christ as risen from the dead and now living and coming between God and us; from their failure to see the things that take place between God and our souls as living, present, and historical.

But the Christian who is enlightened about the resurrection of our Savior enjoys the assurance of his salvation. He is as sure of it as he is sure that Jesus Christ is risen. In order to make him doubt his eternal hope, it would be necessary to begin by making him doubt that Jesus Christ is risen from the dead. That is why the day we are celebrating[1] is the greatest day of the Christian year, and the event we recall today is not *an* event of the kingdom of heaven but *the* event of the kingdom of heaven. It was principally the resurrection of our Savior that the apostles strove to teach.

And we, my friends, let us lay hold of that resurrection; let us live with Jesus Christ risen, and we will enjoy this precious privilege. But at the same time, let us not forget the cost at which that resurrection was attained and the path through which Jesus Christ passed. Let our hearts only savor the gladness of that assurance with a deep feeling of gratitude and love for the one to whom we owe it.

Receive these few words in the love of the Lord, just as I speak them to you (that is all I am able to say to you), and let each of us apply ourselves to develop these thoughts before him in the silence of prayer and in the study of God's Word, at the feet of Jesus Christ risen and in the love of Jesus Christ crucified! Amen.

To read the talks in original
chronological order, go to
the next chapter.

1 Easter, or Resurrection Sunday.

GOD IS LOVE

(March 30, 1856)

Make a joyful shout to the LORD, all you lands!
Serve the LORD with gladness;
Come before his presence with singing.
Know that the LORD, he is God;
It is he who has made us, and not we ourselves;
We are his people, and the sheep of his pasture.

Enter into his gates with thanksgiving,
And into his courts with praise.
Be thankful to him, and bless his name.
For the LORD is good;
His mercy is everlasting,
And his truth endures to all generations.

Psalm 100 NKJV

My dear friends, I am the one who asked our friend to
read us this psalm. I have strength left only to interest my-

self in the love of God. God loved us: that is the entire doctrine of the gospel. Let us love God: that is its entire moral. Scarcely knowing if I will be able to make myself heard, I gather up my small strength to invoke with you the eternal and infinite love of God.

PRAYER

O God, who is love, who has never done, never does, and never will do anything to us except through love, how can I thank you enough on seeing these brothers whom love has gathered around my bed of sickness, of suffering, and of that which you alone can know! I rejoice in their love. To whom has it been better shown? Would I not be the most ungrateful of men if I were not the most grateful? That is why, my God, I give you thanks.

I give you thanks still more, if it is possible, for your love, which has so much afflicted me but also so much sustained me. I confess before them that your love has never left me lacking for any help, though I may often have been lacking in faith and in patience, and though I may still be far from having attained that perfect patience to which I most aspire.

You have been goodness itself, and so long as I still have even a breath of life and of strength I want to confess that fact before them. Your goodness, your goodness! My God, I give you thanks for how gratuitously that goodness is demonstrated in freely pardoning me for all of my faults; me, the chief among sinners, the least of your children, the poorest of your servants; but also me whom you have filled with blessings and used for the advancement of your reign even in the excess of weakness and pain in which I am plunged today!

Oh, how I thank you that you have given me a Savior!

Without him, I confess, oh, my God, that I would be irrevocably lost and in the most awful despair today. But I have a Savior! He has freely saved me through his shed blood, and I want it to be known that I lean uniquely on that poured-out blood. All my righteous acts, all my works that have been praised, all my preaching that has been appreciated and sought after—all that is in my eyes only filthy rags.

I want it to be known that there is nothing in me capable of surviving for one moment before the brightness of your face and before the light of your holiness. But now it is not I who will be judged, it is Christ in me; and I know, I know that he will enter, and I with him, and that he and I are so fully united that he would never enter and leave me outside.

My God, I give you thanks with all these friends, to whom you have granted the same privilege and the same consolation. You have deigned to give the Holy Spirit to them as you have to me, so that he might apply to their souls the free gift of eternal life through the blood of Jesus Christ.

I give you thanks, first of all, for my dear family . . . I give you thanks for my brothers, my sisters, my friends who have all been brothers and sisters to me. These now give testimony through their love and their tears of their tender sympathy, which I have in no way merited and of which I recognize myself to be totally unworthy. Yet you placed it in them for me, and it is such a great consolation to me.

I give you thanks for all things. I thank you for the consolations you have poured out this week. I thank you for the nomination of the professor at Montauban, which has been for us such a great subject of preoccupation and prayer. I thank you for that peace signed just today.[1] We have asked

---

1 The peace treaty ending the Crimean War was signed in Paris in 1856.

you often for that peace, because we think that earthly peace is still a fitting support, as it has been before, for the peace that descends from on high.

It is true, Lord, for I desire to be sincere before you, that I suffer much, and that my joy and my thanksgiving are made somber by these continual sufferings and exhaustion. But you have sustained me up to this point, and I am confident that my prayers and those of my family and friends will win for me perfect patience.

And now, Lord, I take all these friends, and I place them in your fatherly bosom, in the name of Jesus and through the Holy Spirit. May there be none in this room who are not reunited in the eternal dwellings, and may we, being seated at the table of Abraham, Isaac, and Jacob, recall with unmingled joy the day that brings us together!

Oh, my God, sanctify us perfectly, and may all that remains to us of life be employed totally in your service. May your Spirit dwell in us and be the soul, the life, and the joy of us all, of all our families, and of our afflicted ones.

Oh, Lord, many of us have sick ones, sick ones who are very dear to us, and we commend them to you. I carry them all on my heart before you. I do not wish to name them for fear that in my weakness I might forget someone and cause pain to one of those who is here. But I take them all and place them at the foot of the cross of Jesus so that you might comfort and sanctify them.

May your grace and your peace be with us all, from this day forth and forever! Amen.

CHRONOLOGICAL LIST OF TALKS

(WITH ORIGINAL TITLES)

Adolphe Monod (1802–1856) was one of the greatest preachers in the French Reformed Church. He was a pastor of various French congregations, including the prominent Reformed Church of Paris, and a professor at the Reformed Seminary in Montauban. His sermons and essays are popular around the world.

Constance K. Walker (Ph.D. Nuclear Chemistry, University of Rochester) is a Senior Research Scientist at Duke University. She has published more than fifty articles in the field of physics, and has given numerous talks on science and faith.